Dear

God Bless you
on your Confirmati'
May you find
peace and happiness
forever.

Love,
Tita Yollie, Tito
Wallie +
Kuya JR

Following the
Holy Spirit

THE SPIRIT OF TRUTH — Jesus said: "When the Advocate comes, Whom I will send you from the Father, the Spirit of truth Who comes from the Father, He will testify on My behalf. . . . He will guide you into all the truth" (Jn 15:26; 16:13).

Following the Holy Spirit

**DIALOGUES, PRAYERS, and DEVOTIONS
INTENDED TO HELP EVERYONE
KNOW, LOVE, AND FOLLOW
THE HOLY SPIRIT**

By
REV. WALTER VAN DE PUTTE, C.S.SP.

Illustrated by G. Soler

Dedicated to ST. JOSEPH
Patron of the Universal Church

CATHOLIC BOOK PUBLISHING CO.
New York, N.Y.

IMPRIMI POTEST: Philip J. Haggerty, C.S.Sp.,
Provincial

NIHIL OBSTAT: Daniel V. Flynn, J.C.D.
Censor Librorum

IMPRIMATUR: Joseph T. O'Keefe
Vicar General, Archdiocese of New York

(T-335)

PREFACE

MANY questions come to our minds when there is mention of the Holy Spirit. Does He exist? Did He exist from all eternity? What is He, in Himself and in the Holy Trinity? What relationship do we have with Him? What is particularly attributed (by way of "appropriation") to Him? Where can we obtain authentic information about the Holy Spirit, about His activity in us?

What is His role with respect to our supernatural life, to the special means put at our disposal, such as, Sacraments, the Holy Sacrifice of the Mass? What are the "Gifts of the Holy Spirit," the "Fruits of the Holy Spirit"? What are the reasons for a special devotion to the Holy Spirit? In what way should we pray to the Holy Spirit and what should we particularly pray for? Finally: How can we be said to be "FOLLOWING THE HOLY SPIRIT"?

We know that we are called to follow Christ, to imitate Him, as is so well taught in The *Imitation of Christ*. This is a fundamen-

5

tal necessity for a Christian who must strive to become "another Christ" — in accord with the very words of our Lord Himself: "*I am the Way. . . . I have given you an example. What I have done for you, you should also do*" (Jn 14:6; 13:15).

We should also imitate Mary, Mother of Christ and Mother of the Church in all her members. Jesus as Man was always led by the Holy Spirit and was also brought up by Mary. She conceived Jesus by the Holy Spirit and was certainly always led by the Holy Spirit. As we shall see, we too, members of Christ's Mystical Body and children of Mary, must willingly, lovingly, be "following the Holy Spirit."

This is not a treatise of theology of the Holy Spirit. It is a devotional book, intended to help readers to know and love the Holy Spirit, to discern and follow His inspirations. This, at the same time, will make them follow Christ's example more closely, and execute the will of the Heavenly Father more perfectly.

Hence, it is meant to increase our respect and love for the Most Holy Trinity. It should make us more willing to do and suffer all things for the greater glory of God, and to exercise practical love for our neighbor, for

God wants all human beings to be sanctified and to obtain salvation and eternal blessedness with God.

To attain these ends, we recall what the sacred authors of Holy Scripture, under the inspiration of the Holy Spirit, and what Mother Church, Spouse of the Holy Spirit, have said about the Holy Spirit. We also offer some examples of prayers addressed to the Holy Spirit.

In imitation of the precious book called *The Imitation of Christ*, which for a long time was the most cherished spiritual book in the Western Church, we dare to make use of a similar method of "colloquy"—here with the Holy Spirit—regarding some matters of great importance for children of the Father, disciples of Christ, and followers of the Holy Spirit.

May the Sanctifier Blest be pleased to bless this unpretentious work enabling it to some extent to be instrumental in giving to the Church in all her members a truly spiritual renewal so eagerly desired by the successors of St. Peter in our time.

Holy Spirit, fill the hearts of the faithful.

Kindle in them the fire of Your LOVE.

CONTENTS

ST. LUKE INSPIRED WRITER—Under the inspiration of the Holy Spirit, St. Luke composed two books of the New Testament: "The Gospel according to St. Luke" and "The Acts of the Apostles." The second is sometimes called "The Gospel of the Holy Spirit."

10

Chapter 1

ST. LUKE AND THE HOLY SPIRIT

(Imitating the method of the author of *The Imitation of Christ* we here begin colloquies between the Holy Spirit and a Follower of the same Spirit.)

Follower:

WE KNOW, Holy Spirit, that all Scripture is inspired by You. We know also that all the Gospels refer to You and that St. Paul in many Epistles is not forgetful of You. But whom do You consider to be, as it were, Your evangelist?

Luke, we well know, must have been a compassionate physician. Some call him "Our Lady's chronicler" because of what he wrote about the Mother of Jesus.

Holy Spirit:

Though all the Holy Scriptures are equally inspired by Me, it is very true that inspiration does not mean dictating. We leave great liberty to the human. Each one has his own style, his own preferences.

Hence, it is not surprising that the kind physician Luke would have written much about Me Whom you call Comforter, and about Whom you read in the Holy Scriptures that *the love of God has been poured into our hearts through the Holy Spirit Who has been given to us* (Rom 5:5).

Follower:

I realize why the Acts of the Apostles has been called "the Gospel of the Holy Spirit." But when I consult St. Luke, even his Gospel —which like the other Gospels is centered on Jesus Christ—is full of loving references to You.

As I read that Gospel once more I took note of such references. It is foolish to quote them to You Who know them so well, but readers of this colloquy might like to get a sort of bouquet of them.

Luke, evangelist of the Infancy of Jesus, has given us the Golden Gospel of the Annunciation. There we read the dialogue of an Angel, God's messenger, and Mary: . . . *"The Holy Spirit will come upon you [Mary]. . . . Therefore, the Child to be born [of you] will be holy, and He will be called the Son of God."* And Mary, having sufficiently understood her role, said: *"I am the servant of the Lord. Let it be done to me according to your word"* (Lk 1:26-38).

This certainly means, Most Holy Spirit, that Mary conceived Jesus by You; so we like to call Mary the Spouse of the Holy Spirit.

Holy Spirit:

Luke rightly recalls that Mary, instead of remaining home and contemplating her wonderful vocation as Mother of the Divine Savior, immediately acted as a handmaid, as a servant, going to help her cousin Elizabeth who, she had been told, was with child. Mary was truly a Christopher, a Christ-bearer, but you could also call her a Spirit-bearer, for I dwelt in her as in a tabernacle or tent. I dwelt in her from the moment of her conception.

Note that when Mary entered the house of her cousin, the latter *was filled with the Holy Spirit* and exclaimed: *"And why am I so greatly favored that the Mother of my Lord should visit me?"* And you are also told that *the Child in [her] womb leaped for joy* (Lk 1:39-56).

Follower:

Tabernacles, temples of the Holy Spirit, how great a privilege that is! I recall that Pasteur, the famous chemist, when he was received as a member into the French Academy, said in his discourse that the most beautiful word in his language was "enthousiasme," which according to him came from the Greek *"en Theos,"* meaning "God within." For Mary this was literally true: You, Holy Spirit, were truly within her and therefore God was in a wonderful way in Mary.

I also recall that when the parents brought the Holy Child Jesus to Jerusalem to present Him to the Lord, the holy man Simeon, *prompted by the Spirit,* took the Child in his arms, blessed God and recognized in Jesus *a Light for revelation to the Gentiles and glory for [God's] people Israel* (Lk 2:22-35).

Holy Spirit:

If you consider what happened during the public life of Jesus, you will likewise notice that I did not limit My intervention to the time of Jesus' infancy. Jesus, after all, was always the most perfect tabernacle or temple of the Triune God. But for the sake of people from time to time I called attention to My presence.

Follower:

How true that is, Holy Spirit. There is, for instance, that extraordinary humiliation chos-

THE HOLY SPIRIT DESCENDS ON JESUS — "After John had baptized all the people, and while Jesus was engaged in prayer after also having been baptized, heaven opened and the Holy Spirit descended on Him in bodily form like a dove" (Lk 3:21-22).

15

en by Jesus Who wanted to be baptized by John the Baptist as if He were a sinner: *After John had baptized all the people, and while Jesus was engaged in prayer after also having been baptized, . . . the Holy Spirit descended on Him in bodily form like a dove. And a voice came from heaven: "You are My beloved Son"* (Lk 3:21-22).

Holy Spirit:

I sometimes manifest Myself at the beginning and sometimes again at the end. How clearly St. Luke expresses this when he describes the sort of retreat Christ made before beginning His evangelizing work: *Filled with the Holy Spirit, Jesus returned from the Jordan and was led by the Spirit into the desert for forty days* (Lk 4:1).

Chapter 2

A HOLY WITNESSING

Follower:

DEAR Holy Spirit, the Acts of the Apostles is so richly inspired by You and makes Your sanctifying action so well known. On reading this magnificent book once more, I cannot help admiring how well Luke, under Your inspiration and guidance, has witnessed to and for You and at the same time to our Savior Jesus Christ.

Like Paul, Luke had not had the privilege of being one of Christ's seminarians. He had not heard Christ during His public life, nor had he witnessed Christ's Passion and Death or His Ascension. It was by consulting the first Apostles and disciples, perhaps also by interviewing Mary, that he was able to give us such an excellent account of Christ's life upon earth.

Neither was Luke a witness of Your spectacular descent upon the Apostles on the first Pentecost.

In spite of all that, Luke has been successful in honoring You and prompting many who read his testimony to practice a true devotion to You.

I like the way Luke starts his "Gospel of the Holy Spirit": *[Jesus] was taken up into heaven, after first giving instructions through the Holy Spirit to the Apostles whom He had chosen. . . . [and telling them:] "You will receive power when the Holy Spirit comes upon you, and then you will be My witnesses . . . to the farthest corners of the earth"* (Acts 1:1-8).

Witnesses to the Father, to the Son, to You, the Holy Spirit—what a privilege; to be witnesses by word and example to the Creator, to the Redeemer, and to the Sanctifier!

Holy Spirit:

You are right. There is nothing glorious about being a witness in a courtroom when evidence is sought to determine a certain fact.

The Church, your Mother and Teacher, makes you say in the Creed which you recite at Mass: "We believe in the Holy Spirit. . . . He has spoken through the Prophets." This was true for Prophets in the Old Testament. It is also true for the New Testament.

I have never spoken through a voice heard by human ears, nor have I ever been seen with human eyes. You recalled how I "spoke" by appearing like a dove when Jesus was baptized by John. You also noted how through an

Angel I testified that Jesus was conceived of and by Me. I testify by a Light unseen by human eyes, by an inspiration that is unheard and cannot be imagined by people upon earth.

Luke, Paul, and the other authors of Holy Scripture inspired as they are by Me, bear implicit witness to Me as they witness to the One Who remains for you the Way, the Truth, and the Life. Yet many saw and heard Jesus when He was still on earth but failed to accept His testimony, His teaching, and His self-sacrifice for the glory of God and for the salvation of humanity. Seeing is *not* believing. Faith is a gift of God.

Even the Apostles whom Christ had personally trained and who had been so wonderfully instructed by His words and His example still needed additional light, still needed My witnessing to the Divine Savior.

Follower:

Yes, Holy Spirit, I recall what St. Luke tells us in his Gospel: Jesus appeared to the Apostles who became *troubled*; He ate with them, and afterward *opened their minds to understand the Scriptures. And then He said to them, "Thus it is written that the Messiah would suffer and on the third day rise from the*

*dead. . . . You are witnesses to all these things.
. . . Stay here in the city until you have been
clothed with power from on high*" (Lk 24:36-
49).

I know that Jesus thus spoke of You Who
would witness to Him in a truly spectacular
way on Pentecost.

I also recall that, in preparation for Your
extraordinary coming upon the infant
Church, Jesus wanted the Apostles to remain
in Jerusalem, to make what we should like to
call the First Holy Spirit Retreat.

As St. Luke tells us: *[After the Ascension]
they returned to Jerusalem . . . to the upper
room. . . . All of these were constantly engaged
in prayer, together with the women and Mary
the Mother of Jesus* (Acts 1:12-14).

Holy Spirit:

I am glad you recall all this. The Church
will not witness a spiritual renewal without
prayer, persevering prayer. Practice and
preach devotion to Me. Do not merely recite
with your lips but actually believe what is said
in the prayer: "Send forth Your Spirit . . . ; and
You shall renew the face of the earth [the
Church]."

THE COMING OF THE HOLY SPIRIT—"Suddenly there came from heaven a sound similar to that of a violent wind, and it filled the entire house. . . . There appeared to them tongues as of fire, which separated and came to rest on each one of them. All of them were filled with the Holy Spirit" (Acts 2:2-4).

Often read meditatively Luke's account of what happened on the Day of Pentecost (Acts 2:1-13).

Follower:

How greatly I like to ponder the words of Your faithful evangelist St. Luke, dear Spirit, Light of hearts and minds: *When the day of Pentecost arrived, they were assembled together in one place. Suddenly, there came from heaven a sound similar to that of a violent wind. . . . There appeared to them tongues of fire, which separated and came to rest on each one of them. All of them were filled with the Holy Spirit and began to speak in different languages, as the Spirit enabled them to do so.*

Staying at Jerusalem at the time were devout Jews of every nation. . . . They were much confused because each one heard these men speaking his own language. . . . They asked in utter amazement, "Each of us hears them speaking about the marvels God has accomplished. . . . What does this mean?" they asked one another, while a few remarked with a sneer: "They have had too much new wine!" (Acts 2:1-12).

Holy Spirit:

Luke here shows what a good historian he

is, recounting the unpleasant things as well as the inspiring ones.

You probably see why I expressed Myself by using the symbols of a mighty wind and of fire. It is customary to speak of My "inspiration," a mysterious breathing or prompting; and you call Me "Spirit," which means breath.

Fire also is often used to symbolize something spiritual and even supernatural. It can mean great zeal. Luke recalls Jesus' words: "*I have come to spread fire on the earth*" (Lk 12:49); witnesses to Christ and to Me must spread the fire of ardent love for God and all human beings. Members of a Church that is essentially missionary must be fired with a self-sacrificing eagerness to witness to Christ and make as many followers as possible both of Jesus and of Me.

Follower:

Dear Holy Spirit, one thing that made people marvel was that *Jews of every nation under heaven each heard the Apostles speak* his own language. I am wondering how many, or how few, were able to marvel at the extraordinary thing that was taking place in those who had properly received You Who had come to transform them. It is perfectly clear to us that

Peter and the other Apostles, who had shown so much weakness during our Lord's Passion, had now become "other men," willing witnesses ready to sacrifice their mortal lives for Jesus and for You.

How fortunate we are. Although we never saw Jesus and did not witness the extraordinary things that took place at the first Pentecost, we have still learned that on that day there took place the spiritual and supernatural birth of the Church.

Holy Spirit:

You are fortunate. You recall that Jesus said: *"Blessed are those who have not seen and yet have come to believe"* (Jn 20:29). And you must have read recently in Luke's Prologue to the Acts of the Apostles that while the Apostles were with Jesus just before His Ascension, *they asked: "Lord, is this the time when You are going to restore the kingdom to Israel?"* (Acts 1:6). This shows how unspiritual His seminarians still were.

Follower:

It also shows how much they needed Your light, Your inspiration, and Your assistance to become unworldly men, unambitious men, true followers of the Humble Son of Man as Jesus liked to call Himself.

Scientists speak of evolution, which some call transformism. How much greater and more profound is the supernatural transformation that You accomplished on Pentecost! Did not Jesus say to the Apostles before His Ascension: *"John baptized with water, but within a few days you will be baptized with the Holy Spirit"* (Acts 1:5)? Jesus had said similarly to Nicodemus: *"Amen, amen, I say to you, no one can see the Kingdom of God without being born from above. . . . No one can enter the Kingdom of God without being born of water and the Spirit"* (Jn 3:3-5). What a transformation—to be transformed into an adopted child of God!

Holy Spirit:

Let Me call your attention to the fact that Luke whom you rightly call "Our Lady's chronicler," describing the first Pentecostal Retreat, especially mentions Mary: *with the women and Mary the Mother of Jesus* (Acts 1:14).

Why do I say that this is worth noticing? First, Mary in contrast with the Apostles did not need any spiritual transformation. She was always the perfectly faithful "servant of the Lord."

I repeat: why is it important to recall that *Mary, the Mother of Jesus* was there assiduously praying with the Apostles and that on Pentecost she received an outpouring of Charity?

What was Pentecost? The word refers to the fiftieth day following the second day of Passover time. The Christian Pentecost is not a "Feast of the Holy Spirit." The Church has no Feasts in her Calendar that can be called: Feast of the Heavenly Father, Feast of the Eternal Word (Son of God), and Feast of the Holy Spirit.

The Church, as you know, usually celebrates, not the birthday of Saints, but the day of their birth into heaven.

She does celebrate the birthday of Jesus Christ and the birthdays of Mary and John the Baptist. These are the exception.

Now on Pentecost what you celebrate is *the birthday of the Church*, of the Mystical Body of Christ.

And who is the Mother of the Church? None other than Mary, whom you call "Spouse of the Holy Spirit."

Follower:

I can see now what a joyful day the first "Pentecost" must have been for the Mother of Jesus, the Mother of the Church. I recall that Pope Paul VI insisted on calling Mary: "Mother of the Church" during Vatican Council II.

I recall also that in St. Peter's Basilica there is a mosaic that prompts those who look at it to honor her precisely as *Mater Ecclesiae*, that is, Mother of the Church.

Holy Spirit:

It is also proper to recall that Mary at the Annunciation became Mother of Jesus, of Him Who is the Head of the Church, the Head of His Mystical Body. You can therefore say that the Church was also conceived through Me at that same time.

Follower:

Dear Holy Spirit, how well You fulfill what Jesus said about You as reported by the Beloved Disciple St. John: "*When the Spirit of truth comes, He will guide you into all the truth*" (Jn 16:13).

You know that in our time some judges, legislators, and a good number of mothers proclaim legitimate the killing of a human being after he/she has been conceived. To kill a seed is to kill the plant. Some might have suggested to Mary when she was found to be with a Child conceived by You, and feared what Joseph to whom she was betrothed would say and do about that: "Why not get an abortion?"

It dawns on me also that since Nazareth was the town where Jesus was conceived and where the Church was conceived, Mary would at the same time have murdered the Church, the Mystical Body of Christ, if she had followed such evil suggestions.

"Can anything good come from Nazareth?" (Jn 1:46). This deprecating question was asked with reference to Jesus the Nazorean. In reality, the very best came from Nazareth. Not only was an Angel sent by God to a girl of that despised town but You also overshadowed that humble and insignificant girl. Though she was materially poor, she was, as the Angel knew, immaculate from the moment of her own conception and thus *a highly favored daughter of God*, that is, *full of grace* (Lk 1: 28).

If anyone instructed by the Angel or by You had told Mary's neighbors: "That girl is

THE HOLY SPIRIT CONFERRED ON THE DISCI-PLES — "Jesus then came and stood in their midst and said to them, 'Peace be with you.' After saying this, He showed them His hands and His side. The disciples were filled with joy when they saw the Lord. 'Peace be with you,' He said to them again. 'As the Father has sent Me, so I send you.' After this He breathed on them and said, 'Receive the Holy Spirit' " (Jn 20:19-22).

the tabernacle of God, the Mother of the
Messiah, of the King of Kings, the Mother of
God, and the Mother of the Church which
her Son will found," it is not difficult to imagine what those neighbors would have said. In
our day such a Mary might have been relegat-
ed to a mental hospital.

Holy Spirit:

Speaking once more about the true meaning of the Christian Feast of Pentecost, you
might ask yourself why Jesus chose that particular Jewish Feast Day.

Recall that devout Jews had come from all
nations. It was in a sense a universal feast. You
see directly how proper it is to celebrate the
birthday, on this Feast Day, of the Church of
Christ designated by the word Catholic,
which, precisely, means universal. Jerusalem
on that first Pentecost became as it were the
center of an explosion that was destined to
affect all the peoples of the earth.

Jesus could have given the fullness of the
Holy Spirit to the Apostles before His
Ascension. He could have done so on the very
day of His Resurrection. In fact, He gave Me
to the Apostles gathered in an upstairs room:
He breathed on them and said, "Receive the

Holy Spirit. If you forgive the sins of anyone, they are forgiven" (Jn 20:22-23). He thus gave them the wonderful power of reconciling sinners with God.

Jesus had said twice before: *"Peace be with you."* The King of Peace gave Me to His Apostles that they in turn might become peacemakers. But, I repeat once more, He did not want then and there to give the Apostles the great enlightenment and ardent zeal that was bestowed on the Apostles after their Pentecostal Retreat, that is, the fullness of the Holy Spirit.

My role is to give an all-embracing and persevering animation to the Church that must continue the work of the Son of Man, the Divine Savior, until the end of time. Hence, the birth of Christ's Mystical Body on Pentecost was the beginning of a mission of the Spirit in the Church, a mission of inspiration of the community of faith, for the sake of a universal, a catholic witnessing to the Trinity: Father, Son and Holy Spirit.

Chapter 3

PAUL, FOLLOWER OF THE HOLY SPIRIT

Follower:

D EAR Holy Spirit, we have spoken about
St. Luke and his evident devotion toward
You, which is clearly expressed already in his
Gospel and then fully in the Acts of the
Apostles, a sort of "Gospel of the Holy Spirit."
I would now like, under Your guidance, to see
whether St. Paul was also an outstanding
"follower" of You.

In all his writings Paul manifests his devotion to Christ: *I . . . know nothing except
Jesus Christ—and Him crucified* (1 Cor 2:2)
became his motto. *Again: The life I live now
is not my own; Christ is living in me* (Gal 2:
20); and again: *Be imitators of me, as I am of
Christ* (1 Cor 11:1).

Holy Spirit:

Human beings cannot see or think of many
things at the same time. God, on the contrary,
Father, Son, and Holy Spirit, knows all things
at the same time and the knowledge of one
Divine Person is as all-embracing as that of the
other two Persons.

True devotion to one Divine Person does not exclude devotion to the other Divine Persons. The fact that the Church addresses most of her prayers to the Heavenly Father does not detract from the Son and from Me.

Follower:

We have also been taught that true devotion to Mary really tends Christward and Godward. And I recall how Luke, in a certain way a biographer of Yours in Acts, chapters 9— 28, is equally pictured as Your Follower and Follower of Jesus Christ.

Holy Spirit:

That is correct. Take, for instance, the way Luke (in chapter 9) describes Saul's conversion.

Follower:

Yes, I remember. Saul was certainly not animated by Your spirit before that wonderful conversion. Breathing vengeance against the Christians, he was suddenly cast down and blinded by Jesus the Lord. And the Lord told Ananias to go to see that former persecutor of followers of Jesus. Ananias went and told Saul: "Saul, *my brother*, [*I have been sent*] . . . *so that you may regain your sight*

*and be filled with the Holy Spirit."
Immediately, . . . [Saul] regained his sight . . .
and was baptized*—that is, he was *begotten of
water and Spirit* (Acts 17-19).

Holy Spirit:

Of course, it is one thing to be baptized but
another to become and remain a true follower
of Jesus, a true follower of Me.

Follower:

I wonder how many of the approximately
three thousand people who were converted at
the first Pentecost persevered in faithfully following You and Christ. I see also that Luke
and Paul did not have the benefit of witnessing
Your spectacular coming in souls on the first
Pentecost—although Saul's conversion was
spectacular enough! Blinded on the road to
Damascus, he soon afterward was filled with
Your *light*, O Holy Spirit.

It is strange that Saul was not converted
when he witnessed the martyrdom of Stephen
the first adult who laid down his life for the
Divine Master. What a horrible prejudice Saul
had against Jesus and against followers of Jesus.

Saul was present at Stephen's discourse and
heard him say: *"You stiff-necked people, . . .*

You are always resisting the Holy Spirit, just as your ancestors used to do." He witnessed the stoning of Stephen and heard him voice forgiveness aloud: *"Lord, do not hold this sin against them"* (Acts 7:51-60). But Saul remained obstinate, spiritually blind.

In our own day, how many there are also who refuse to follow Christ even when they know Him sufficiently. From such blindness, deliver us, Holy Spirit!

Paul's Transformation

Follower:

O NE thing stands out very clearly as we read Luke's account of the extraordinary way Paul was called to be an Apostle. What a *transformation* he underwent! Although it found expression in his words and conduct, it was principally supernatural, hence invisible.

The arch-liar, Satan, told Eve that by eating the forbidden fruit, by disobedience, she and Adam would be transformed into "gods." The same Fallen Angel suggested to Jesus to transform stones into bread. How sensible this was, if Christ had the power to do such things, now that He was exhausted by fasting!

But there are transformations, changes, much more wonderful than that, changes willed by God. As St. John tells us in the Prologue to his Gospel: Jesus empowered those who accepted Him *to become children of God . . . from God Himself* (Jn 1:12-13).

Holy Spirit:

And read further in St. John. There you will find Jesus saying: "*No one can see the Kingdom of God without being born from above. . . . No one can enter the Kingdom of God without being born of water and the Spirit*" (Jn 3:3-5).

Think also of the supernatural change worked by Jesus in the sinful Samaritan woman. She was transformed into a follower of Jesus, into an evangelist of Jesus. Continue to read in St. John.

Follower:

I also remember a wonderful change, a visible one, however, at the wedding feast of Cana, at the request of the Mother of Jesus. He changed water into wine and as a result *his disciples believed in Him* (Jn 2:11).

Then there is the promise of a most extraordinary change, one unperceived by the

THE HOLY SPIRIT GIVES NEW BIRTH—"Jesus replied [to Nicodemus], 'Amen, amen, I say to you, no one can see the Kingdom of God without being born from above.' Nicodemus asked, 'How can a man be born again once he is old?'. . . 'Amen, amen, I say to you, no one can enter the Kingdom of God without being born of water and the Spirit' " (Jn 3:3-6).

senses: "Take this and eat; this is My Body" (Mt 26:26). This promise is given in the inspiring sixth chapter of John's Gospel.

Jesus had multiplied bread for the body. He had compassion on the hungry multitude. We assimilate food, make some of it part of ourselves. Christ gives us food that makes us more like Himself: *"I am the living Bread that came down from heaven. Whoever eats this Bread will live forever; and the Bread that I will give is My Flesh, for the life of the world. . . . My Flesh is real food, and My Blood is real drink"* (Jn 6:51-55).

The Church has considered it good to call the change of bread and wine into Christ's Body and Blood, not "transformation" but "transubstantiation." Through this wonderful change we can receive our Lord, our glorified Lord, so well described by St. Thomas Aquinas:

"O Sacred Banquet, in which Christ is received, the memory of His Passion is recalled, the mind is filled with grace, and we receive a pledge of future glory."

Chesterton said he would not accept a God Whom he (on earth) fully understood. God must be extraordinary and most mysterious to us who rely so very much on sense perception for our thoughts.

Paul Transformed into a Missionary Priest

Holy Spirit:

YOU will do well to recall how "I spoke" to Barnabas and Paul. This took place at Antioch of Syria where followers of Christ were called Christians, where Peter preached as did Saul and Barnabas. So, why not recall what Luke has to say about that (Acts 13:1-12)?

Follower:

One thing that I like to recall in relation to You, Holy Spirit, is this: *On one occasion, while [Barnabas and Saul] were worshiping the Lord and fasting, the Holy Spirit said, "Set Barnabas and Saul apart for Me to do the work to which I have called them." Then, after completing their fasting and prayer, [the prophets of Antioch] laid their hands on them and sent them off* (Acts 13:2-3).

We know that prayer and the *imposition of hands* were characteristic of *ordinations.* Thus, Paul told Timothy whom he had ordained as a bishop to *fan into flame the gift of God that is within you through the laying on of my hands* (2 Tim 1:6).

A bit later in Acts, Luke tells us that Saul *(also known as Paul) was filled with the Holy Spirit* when he severely reprimanded the magician Elymas who opposed Paul and Barnabas. Paul certainly could use strong language when he considered it necessary. He said:

You offspring of the devil, you enemy of righteousness, filled with every kind of deceit and fraud. . . . You will be blind, and for a period of time you will not be able to see the sun" (Acts 13:10-11).

Paul Brings a Kind of Pentecost

Holy Spirit:

WHY not recall what happened at Ephesus, where some disciples had not so *much as heard that there is a Holy Spirit?* They had been baptized with the baptism of repentance administered by John the Baptist.

When things had been properly explained to them, they were baptized in the name of the Lord Jesus: *When Paul laid his hands on them, the Holy Spirit came down upon them and they spoke in tongues and prophesied* (Acts 19:1-10).

Paul Truly Animated by the Holy Spirit

Follower:

I WOULD like to say a word now about the way St. Paul manifested himself to be as it were "another Christ," an imitator of Christ, and at the same time one truly animated by You, Holy Spirit.

Luke tells us (Acts 20:16ff) that Paul *was eager to be in Jerusalem, if possible, on the day of Pentecost.* He sent word to the presbyters of Ephesus that he wanted to see them. And when they had arrived he gave them this wonderful discourse:

"You yourselves know how I lived among you. . . . I served the Lord with all humility and with tears, enduring the trials that came to me as a result of the intrigues of the Jews. I did not hesitate to tell you what was for your benefit as I proclaimed the word to you and taught you publicly as well as in your individual homes. I have insisted to Jews and Gentiles alike about the necessity of repentance before God and faith in our Lord Jesus.

"And now, compelled by the Spirit, I am on my way to Jerusalem without the slightest idea what will happen to me there, except that in every city the Holy Spirit warns me that I will face imprisonment and hardships.

"As for me, I do not regard my life as of any value. I only wish to finish the race and complete the mission that I received from the Lord Jesus, that of bearing witness to the Gospel of God's grace. . . . I did not shrink from proclaiming to you the entire plan of God. Keep watch over yourselves and over all the flock of which the Holy Spirit has made you overseers."

Holy Spirit:

Paul certainly has been a most faithful servant of the Divine Master Who chose to become a servant. Him he has imitated, loving to be *compelled by the Spirit.*

Chapter 4

PENTECOSTAL LESSONS

Follower:

S ANCTIFYING Spirit, I would like to talk with You about what we can learn from Your coming on the first Pentecost. Luke enthusiastically describes what the Apostles and many others learned on that occasion.

Peter was looked upon, no doubt, as an ignorant fisherman. Now, evidently inspired by You, he boldly and confidently stood up with the Eleven and addressed the crowd, explaining what had happened. He recalled that Jesus the Nazorean had been murdered but then had risen from the dead: *"God raised this Jesus to life. Of that we are all witnesses. Exalted at God's right hand, He received from the Father the promise of the Holy Spirit and has poured [the Spirit] out on us. . . . Therefore, let the whole house of Israel know with complete certitude that God has made this Jesus Whom you crucified both Lord and Messiah"* (Acts 2:32-33, 36).

Strange! No one took up stones to kill Simon Peter, crying out: He has blasphemed.

On the contrary, the hearers were *deeply shaken*. They asked Peter and the other Apostles, *"What are we to do, brothers?"* Peter answered: *Repent and be baptized, . . . so that your sins may be forgiven, and you will receive the gift of the Holy Spirit."* The result? Some three thousand were added that day to the Church of Christ (Acts 2:37-41) What a miraculous growth of the "Infant Church"!

Holy Spirit:

You reported well what Peter, Head of the Church, said on that glorious day. You know that you must always beware of sudden feelings of enthusiasm. There were great conversions on Pentecost and for many days, weeks, and months afterward.

People remain weak even when great graces are given to them. They are in need of persevering prayer, like that practiced by the Apostles with Mary before Pentecost. They prayed with humble confidence in God, refusing to rely solely on themselves. These are fundamentals for fallen people even when they have received great graces on "a Pentecost."

During the Passion Peter had been too self-reliant and failed miserably regarding his promise of fidelity. Even after Pentecost, as Paul recalls in Galatians (2:11-14), Peter showed weakness in the way he dealt with the Judaizers. Life upon earth remains a "spiritual combat" as one Christian writer has expressed it.

Prayer in and to the Holy Spirit

Follower:

DEAR Divine Teacher, some people wonder why Luke and Paul, and Jesus also, insist so much on the necessity of praying—not only at times such as the "novena" before Pentecost, when the Apostles with Mary together devoted themselves to *constant prayer*, but *always*, as Jesus taught (Lk 18:1), and as Paul was fond of repeating (1 Thes 5:17).

I know they did not mean that vocal prayers have to be recited all day long. Christ, Mary, and Paul did not do that. But I feel certain that the Apostles after receiving You at Pentecost were living in constant loving union with You, which means with the Father and the Son also. They did and suffered all things for God's greater glory and for the sanctification and salvation of themselves and all others.

Good Christian parents cannot say vocal prayers all day long. But with devotedness to our Lady and to You, they strive to do and suffer all things out of love for God and for the members of their family. They thus "pray constantly."

Holy Spirit:

You interpret well the demand for constant prayer, for "praying always." People on earth are not in a heavenly condition. In heaven nothing distracts Angels and Saints from living constantly in loving union with God. People on earth must engage in all kinds of work.

Some, unfortunately, lose themselves so much in earthly affairs that they forget to thank God, and neglect to ask for His help, a help so necessary if they want to live good lives. Others become wholly self-reliant and pursue only earthly goals, seeking happiness where they will not find it.

Follower:

We know that there was no danger of Jesus as Man committing sin and offending His Heavenly Father. It was not absolutely necessary for Him to be led by You into the desert to make a sort of retreat before engaging in His public ministry. Neither was it necessary for Him to pray before choosing His Apostles, as Luke recalls He did.

We see clearly that He did such things to teach us to withdraw now and then from worldly occupations and commune with God in prayer.

Holy Spirit:

Wise spiritual authors rightly advise people to renew their spiritual intentions from time to time, for instance, to say a prayer before any work, asking the Holy Spirit to help them. In addition, people should immediately pray when tempted to offend God by sin.

Morning and evening prayers, examination of conscience, really trying to do all things for the greater glory of God, and sincerely renewing such an intention from time to time: these are valuable means for growth in holiness.

Follower:

We have no excuse for omitting prayer. Many are the occasions when we are virtually asked to pray. For example, we hear that someone has died. It matters not whether he or she was a friend or even an enemy (*"Pray for those who persecute you"*—Mt 5:44). Why not say (part of) the Rosary for such a person. This, I am sure, Holy Spirit, You virtually tell us.

PRAYER FOR OTHERS IN THE SPIRIT—"Jesus answered him, . . . 'The Holy Spirit, Whom the Father will send in My name, will teach you everything. . . . If you ask the Father for anything in My name, He will give it to you. . . . Pray for those who persecute you' " (Jn 14:22, 26; 16:23; Mt 5:44).

How privileged some of us have been to have learned to pray "at our mother's knee." How sad, as sometimes happens, when we tell someone who has told us about his or her sufferings and sorrows: "Why not pray?" And he or she answers: "How do you do that?"

Holy Spirit:

Tell people to recite and sometimes meditate on the prayers found in Holy Scripture. If they are Catholics, tell them to meditate also on some of the prayers Mother Church proposes for Mass and the Liturgy of the Hours, for instance, the Prayer of the Faithful. There are many inspiring prayers composed by Popes, Bishops, priests, by Saints belonging to any and every class of society.

A child knows what things to ask for and in what way to ask for them. Children of an infinitely good Father in heaven surely should find it easy to ask for what they need; but it is proper always to add: "If this is in line with Your Holy Will, O Lord."

Follower:

We have been told that prayer is very simple: a familiar conversation with God Who, we know, loves us. What I have been doing, dear Holy Spirit, has in fact been such a familiar conversation with You: a *prayer*. And by printing *colloquies* with the Holy Spirit perhaps I have been helping people to pray.

Besides that, I have found it useful to offer a selection of prayers from time to time, some of which might inspire the readers to pray "led by the Holy Spirit."

Chapter 5

A SELECTION OF PRAYERS

The Lord's Prayer

OUR FATHER, Who art in heaven, hallowed be Thy Name; Thy Kingdom come; Thy will be done on earth as it is in heaven.

Give us this day our daily bread, and forgive us our trespasses as we forgive those who trespass against us, and lead us not into temptation, but deliver us from evil. Amen.

The Hail Mary

HAIL Mary, full of grace, the Lord is with thee. Blessed art thou among women; and blessed is the fruit of thy womb, Jesus.

Holy Mary, Mother of God, pray for us, sinners, now and at the hour of our death. Amen.

An Act of Faith

O MY God, I firmly believe all the sacred truths that Your Holy Church believes and teaches, because You have revealed them, Who can neither deceive nor be deceived. Amen.

An Act of Hope

O MY God, relying on Your infinite goodness and promises, I hope to obtain the pardon of my sins, the assistance of Your grace, and life everlasting, through the merits of Jesus Christ, our Lord and Redeemer. Amen.

An Act of Love

O MY God, I am heartily sorry for having offended You. I hate and detest all my sins because I fear the loss of heaven and the pains of hell, but most of all because I love You, my God, Who are infinitely perfect and worthy of all my love. Amen.

(Being sorry for our sins because of such perfect love of God Who is infinite goodness, can be called *"an insurance for eternal life."* It is most useful to make such an act of perfect contrition as soon as possible after committing a mortal sin.)

Prayer to Mary

O HOLY Virgin, Mother of God, my advocate and patroness, I place myself under your protection and cast myself with confidence into the bosom of your mercy.

Be, O good Mother, my refuge in my necessities, my consolation in my pains, and my advocate with your Divine Son now, and especially at the hour of my death. Amen.

Prayer to Our Guardian Angel

BLESSED spirit, my Guardian Angel, whom God has appointed to watch over me, intercede for me this day, that I may not stray from the path of virtue. Amen.

Prayer to the Saints

SAINT Joseph, holy Apostles, and all our holy Patron Saints, intercede for me, that I may serve God faithfully in this life as you have done, and glorify Him eternally with you in heaven. Amen.

The Magnificat: Canticle of Mary

MY SOUL proclaims the greatness of the Lord,
   and my spirit rejoices in God my Savior.
For He has looked with favor on the lowliness of His servant;
   henceforth all generations will call me blessed.
The Mighty One has done great things for me,
   and holy is His Name;
His mercy is shown from age to age
   on those who fear Him.

He has shown the strength of His arm,
  He has routed those who are arrogant in
    mind and heart.
He has brought down monarchs from their
    thrones
  and lifted up the lowly.
He has filled the hungry with good things
  and sent the rich away empty.
He has come to the aid of Israel His servant,
  ever mindful of His merciful love,
according to the promises He made to our
    ancestors,
  to Abraham and to his descendants forever
                    (Lk 1:46-55).

(This prayerful Canticle is recited by millions every day. Mary continues to be loved and honored, and honoring her is to honor God Who chose her to be Mother of the Savior, Mother of the Church.)

1—3. Prayer to the Holy Spirit

MOST loving Lord mercifully listen to our prayers. Enlighten us by the grace of the Holy Spirit. Enable us to participate in the Holy Sacrifice of the Mass with gratitude and a desire to serve You better.

COME, Holy Spirit, fill the hearts of the faithful and kindle in them the fire of Your love.

Send forth Your Spirit and they shall be created.

And You shall renew the face of the earth.

O GOD, Who have instructed the hearts of the faithful by the Light of the Holy Spirit, grant by the same Spirit that we may relish what is right and always enjoy His consolation. Amen.

4. Jesus, Send Your Spirit

HELP me to spread Thy fragrance everywhere.
Flood my soul with Thy Spirit and Life.
Penetrate and possess my whole being,
So utterly that all my life may be
Only a radiance of Thine.

Shine through me, and be so in me,
That every soul I come in contact with
May feel Thy presence in my soul.
Let them look up and no longer see
But only Jesus.   (Cardinal Newman)

5. Lead, Kindly Light

LEAD, kindly Light, amid the encircling gloom,
Lead Thou me on;
The night is dark, and I am far from home,

Lead Thou me on.
Keep Thou my feet; I do not ask to see
The distant scene; one step enough for me.

I was not ever thus, nor prayed that Thou
Shouldst lead me on;
I loved to choose and see my path; but now
Lead Thou me on.
I loved the garish day, and, spite of fears,
Pride ruled my will: remember not past years.

So long Thy power hath blest me, sure it still
Will lead me on
O'er moor and fen, o'er crag and torrent, till
The night is gone,
And with the morn those Angel faces smile,
Which I have loved long since, and lost
    awhile.   (Cardinal Newman)

6. Short Prayer to the Holy Spirit

COME, Holy Spirit,
    Come, Divine Love,
Who once appeared
    Resembling a Dove.
Come, Lord of Light,
    And Fire Divine,
Come with Your Might
    In hearts like mine.
Faith now is weak,
    Priests? They are few.

May many seek
  To follow You!

7. Morning Prayer to the Holy Spirit

ALMIGHTY and eternal God, Who at the
third hour poured out Your Holy Spirit
into the Apostles, send forth also into us the
same Spirit of Love so that we may faithfully
give testimony to You before all human
beings. Through Christ our Lord. Amen.

8. Another Prayer to Receive the Holy Spirit

O KING of glory, send us the Promised of
the Father, the Spirit of Truth. May the
Counselor Who proceeds from You enlighten us and infuse all truth into us, as You have
promised.

O Father of our Lord Jesus Christ, grant
that Christ by faith may dwell in our hearts
so that, rooted in charity, we may acknowledge the love of Christ that surpasses all
knowledge. Through the same Christ our
Lord. Amen.

9. Prayer for the Seven Gifts of the Holy Spirit

O LORD Jesus Christ, before ascending into
heaven You promised to send the Holy
Spirit to continue Your work in the souls of

the Apostles and disciples. Grant the same Spirit to us that we may ever better cooperate with Your love and grace.

Grant us the spirit of *Wisdom*—that we may not unduly attach ourselves to perishable things and aspire ever more for things that are eternal. The spirit of *Understanding*—that Divine Truth might enlighten our mind. The spirit of *knowledge*—that we may see all things in the light of Divine Revelation. The spirit of *Counsel*—that we may always choose the surest way of pleasing God. The spirit of *Fortitude*—that we may bear our crosses with courage. The Spirit of *Piety*—that we may be filled with a childlike love for God and be eager to obey Him in all things. The spirit of *Fear*—that will make us avoid whatever displeases You. This we ask, for the greater glory of the Triune God. Amen.

(Fr. Lechner, C.S.Sp.)

10. Prayer of St. Augustine

HOLY Spirit, powerful Consoler, sacred Bond of the Father and the Son, Hope of the afflicted, descend in my heart and establish in it Your loving dominion. Enkindle in my tepid soul the fire of Your Love so that I may be wholly subject to You.

We believe that when You dwell in us, You also prepare a dwelling for the Father and the Son. Deign, therefore, to come to me, Consoler of abandoned souls. Protector of those in need, help the afflicted, strengthen the weak, support the wavering.

Come and purify me. Suffer no evil desire to take possession of me. You love the humble and resist the proud. Come to me, glory of the living, hope of the dying. Lead me by Your grace that I may always be pleasing to You. Amen.

11. Prayer of Leo XIII

O HOLY Spirit, Creator, generously help the Catholic Church. By Your supernatural power strengthen and confirm her against the assaults of the enemy. By Your Love and grace renew the spirit of Your servants whom You have animated—that in You they may glorify also the Father and His only Son, our Lord. Amen.

12. Prayer of St. Pius X

O HOLY Spirit of Light and Love, to You I consecrate my mind, heart, and will, for time and eternity. May I be ever docile to Your Divine inspirations and to the teachings of the Holy Catholic Church whose infallible Guide You are.

May my heart be ever inflamed with the love of God and love of neighbor; may my will be ever in harmony with Your Divine will. May my life faithfully imitate the life and virtues of our Lord and Savior Jesus Christ. To Him with the Father and You, Divine Spirit, be honor and glory forever. Amen.

13. The Secret of Sanctity

(During a retreat, Cardinal Mercier (d. 1926) was asked by one of the retreatants to reveal what is "the secret of sanctity." This took place at the convent of the Religious of the Sacred Heart, Brussels. Here is his answer:)

EVERY day, for five minutes restrain your imagination; close your eyes, as it were, and your ears, to all earthly impressions so as to be able to withdraw into the sanctuary of your baptized soul, the temple of the Holy Spirit. Then address to the Holy Spirit words like these:

O Holy Spirit, Soul of my soul, I adore You. Enlighten, guide, strengthen, console me.

Tell me what I ought to do.
I promise to be submissive to You in every-
    thing
that You will ask of me.
I promise to accept whatever You will permit
to befall me.
Merely show me what is Your Will.

If you do this, you will spend your life in
contentment and peace. You will have abundant consolation even amidst troubles, for
you will receive grace in proportion to your
burdens, until the day when you will reach
heaven weighted with precious merits.

This submission to the Holy Spirit can be
called: *the secret of sanctity.*

Chapter 6

PRAYERS OF PETITION

Follower:

I FEEL sorry for so many men and women today who live as if they had no Father in heaven, no intercessors of whom the greatest is Jesus Christ, and no Holy Spirit Who is always ready to enlighten, comfort, console, guide, and inspire faith and confidence as well as love for God and neighbor.

Children most naturally ask for things from their parents and thereby virtually confess their dependence on them. How is it possible for us, children of God, especially when we have been adopted by God as "Children of God," not to ask for the things that God knows to be good for us for time and for eternity?

When this is done in the proper spirit, we realize that asking in this way is an acknowledgment of our dependence on God and the necessity of being submissive to Him. At the same time, it helps us really mean it when we say, as Christ taught us: "Hallowed be Thy Name. Thy Kingdom come. Thy will be done on earth as it is in heaven."

Holy Spirit:

You are right in stating that people should ask for things from God. Jesus said insistently: *"Ask, and you will receive"* (Mt 7:7). Luke also recalls how Jesus taught His disciples to ask for things, and to ask for things in their proper order (Lk 11:9-13).

Follower:

I notice that he gives a short form of the Our Father (Lk 11:2-4) but the essentials are there: We first must ask: *"Father, hallowed be Your Name. Your Kingdom come."* Then we can add petitions for our well-being: *"Give us each our daily bread. And forgive us our sins. . . . And do not lead us into temptation."*

Holy Spirit:

Children sometimes constantly ask for things in a purely selfish way. There are also Christians who pray only when they find no help in human beings and then demand that what they ask be granted. If God fails to grant precisely what they have requested, some may stop praying altogether.

It is important to remember that there are other very important kinds of prayer—prayers of "giving": giving thanks, giving glory and

JESUS ENCOURAGES PRAYER OF PETITION —
"Therefore, I say to you: ask, and it will be given you;
seek, and you will find; knock, and the door will be
opened to you. . . . If you, then, despite your evil
nature, know how to give good gifts to your children,
how much more will the heavenly Father give the Holy
Spirit to those who ask Him" (Lk 11:9-13)?

honor to God, offering spiritual sacrifices, and doing penance for our sins. There is also the prayer of forgiving others which is a fundamental kind of prayer: *"Forgive us our sins, for we ourselves forgive everyone who is in debt to us"* (Lk 11:4).

Follower:

Dear Spirit of Love, is there not also a superior kind of prayer of petition when we pray for others? Some of us speak of the apostolate of prayer. Many good Christians have an ever increasing list of "others" for whom they want to pray—at Mass, when praying the Rosary, during visits to the Blessed Sacrament, or to the Sacred Heart, Our Lady, St. Joseph, or some other Saint.

Holy Spirit:

You are right. Exemplary in that practice are many cloistered nuns, such as Carmelites and Poor Clares, whose monasteries are powerhouses of intercessory prayer. They do not need any broadcasting apparatus to send out their petitions to God, nor do those for whom they pray require a radio or a television in order to reap the benefit of such supernatural broadcasting.

The models of these nuns are Jesus the greatest of Intercessors and the Blessed Mother Mary. Jesus is also rightly called the Mediator, the go-between, the Pontifex (bridge-builder). He is a God-Man, a perfect Mediator in His redeeming action and in His prayer.

He virtually expressed His role as Intercessor, Mediator, and Redeemer when just before His Death on a Cross, hanging "between heaven and earth," He loudly uttered an intercessory prayer saying: *"Father, forgive them, for they do not know what they are doing"* (Lk 23:34).

Follower:

How inspiring such examples of intercessory prayer are, Divine Spirit, inspirer of a truly spiritual renewal of the Church, a spiritual renewal of clergy and laity.

What a pity that too many fail to keep in mind the most consoling truth that You Yourself are an *Intercessor*. Paul, companion of Luke, emphasized this in his wonderful Epistle to the Romans:

The Spirit helps us in our weakness. For we do not know how to pray as we should, but the Spirit Himself intercedes for us with sighs that cannot be put into words. And the One

*Who searches hearts knows the mind of the
Spirit, because the Spirit intercedes for the
saints [Christians] in accordance with God's
will* (Rom 8:26-27).

Holy Spirit:

Christians too must be intercessors; they
must exercise the apostolate of intercession.
Those who are ill, those who are unable to
say long prayers, can offer their sufferings and
intentions of intercession.

If they only knew how powerful are the
intercessions of those who are weakened by
illness, who are as helpless as Jesus when He
was nailed to the Cross and there gave the
perfect example of intercession in intention,
in words, in vicarious sufferings, and in vicarious satisfaction for the sins of humankind.

Learn from Mother Church, a Teacher at
all times, what are the principal things for
which to pray. Learn from her for whom you
should pray frequently, habitually. This will
at the same time be a true joy for you, for
when done in the right spirit intercessory
prayer is charitable giving, and as Jesus said:
"It is more blessed to give than to receive"
(Acts 20:35). This is one reason why Jesus was
the happiest Man Who ever lived. It is also

one reason why Mary was the happiest woman who ever lived. Think of her loving intercession at Cana. Think of her intercessions manifested so clearly at many places where sanctuaries of prayer have been erected. Think of Guadalupe, Lourdes, Fatima, Knock—to mention only a few.

Follower:

Certainly Mother Church is also a Model intercessor; for instance, in the Liturgy of the Mass she suggests for whom we should pray: for the living and the dead, for the Church, for Pope, Bishops, and Priests, for religious, for parents and children, for civil authorities, for the Missions, for vocations, for the sick, for sinners. The list is endless.

It might be useful for the readers of this book to be able to read a few prayers of petition, of intercession "for others." These will be found in the next chapter.

Chapter 7

PRAYERS FOR OTHERS

1. Prayer for the Deceased

O GOD, You are infinite goodness and mercy; grant to N . . . forgiveness of sins and eternal happiness with You in heaven. We ask this through Jesus Christ our Savior and the Holy Spirit, the Consoler. Amen.

2. Prayer for Final Perseverance

HOLY Spirit, what is more important for all human beings than that they should have the privilege of dying a good death, that they should die in Your friendship. Make all die with perfect contrition for their sins. Grant that all may strive for holiness in their short life upon earth, for Your glory and for their eternal happiness with You. Amen.

3. Prayer for Sick Persons

HOLY Spirit, Consoler and Comforter, grant to N . . . recovery from their illness. Grant them health of mind and body in accord with what You consider best for their sanctification and eternal blessedness. If their illness is a cross that You want them to bear, teach them to accept it as followers of Jesus Christ Who suffered and died for us.

It is through You, Holy Spirit, that Jesus offered Himself as a victim of sacrifice. Prompt the sick to repeat Christ's words: *"Not my will but Yours be done"* (Lk 22:42). Amen.

4. Prayer of Parents for Their Children

HEAVENLY Father, You have deigned to bless our sacred union with children. Grant us the grace to teach them by word and example, that they may truly be called your children and resemble Your Son ever more.

Holy Spirit, Spouse of Mary, by Whom she conceived Jesus, inspire us, parents, in our efforts to educate our children in the fundamental art of loving God and neighbor, in obedience to parents and teachers, and in respect for all lawful authority. Amen.

5. Prayer for Our Parents

HOLY Spirit, Spouse of the Blessed Mother Mary, grant me the gift of piety that will make me be devoted to my parents, always honoring them, showing gratitude to them, helping them in their needs. Bless them here below and reward them in heaven.

THE CHURCH REPRESENTS JESUS—"The Lord appointed seventy-two others and sent them on ahead in pairs to every town and place He intended to visit. He said to them: . . . 'Whoever listens to you listens to Me, and whoever rejects you rejects Me. And whoever rejects Me rejects the One Who sent Me' " (Lk 10:1-2, 16).

Let me never forget that Jesus, Son of God and Son of Mary, was obedient to His earthly parents and that, when dying on the Cross, He entrusted His mother to John, the Beloved disciple. Help me to be always grateful to those who were chosen by You to make me Your child for all eternity. Amen.

6. Prayer for Unbelievers

HOLY Spirit, on the first Pentecost, through Your inspiration many were transformed, becoming adopted children of God and faithful disciples of Jesus Christ. They were animated by the love of God that is poured into our souls by the Holy Spirit Who is given to us.

Enlighten the minds of unbelievers, incline their wills to accept the Good News, and prompt them to be obedient to the Teachers of the Church about whom Christ said: *"Whoever listens to you listens to Me, and whoever rejects you rejects Me"* (Lk 10:16).

Teach them how to pray and prepare their minds and hearts for Your coming into their souls. Amen.

7. Prayer of St. Bonaventure

O LORD Jesus, through You I humbly beseech the merciful Father to send the

Holy Spirit of grace, that He may bestow upon human beings His sevenfold Gifts.

May He send them the gift of *wisdom*, which will make them relish the Tree of Life that is no other than *Yourself*; the gift of *understanding*, which will enlighten them; the gift of *counsel*, which will guide them in the way of righteousness; and the gift of *fortitude*, which will give them the strength to vanquish the enemies of their sanctification and salvation.

May He give them the gift of *knowledge*, which will enable them to discern Your teaching and distinguish good from evil; the gift of *piety*, which will make them enjoy true peace; and the gift of *fear*, which will make them shun all iniquity and avoid all danger of offending Your Majesty. To the Father and to the Son and to the Holy Spirit be given all glory and thanksgiving forever. Amen.

8. Prayer for the Propagation of the Faith

O HOLY Spirit, You desire the salvation of all human beings and for that purpose want them all to acquire the knowledge of Your Truth. Grant to all of them Your powerful Light and Your Love of Goodwill that they may give glory to God in unity of faith, hope, and love.

Send laborers into the harvest who are truly animated by You Who are the Soul of the Missionary Church. Amen.

9. Prayer of Husband and Wife

O HOLY Spirit, Spirit of *unity*, Who are the Love and Goodwill of Father and Son, You have made us one in the sacred union of marriage. Grant that, like the first Christians, we may be one heart and one mind.

Make us respect one another, help one another in our striving for holiness, and support one another. Be our Guide, our Counselor, and our Consoler. Make us bear one another's burdens during our journey to heaven where we hope to live forever as adopted children of the Triune God. Amen.

10. Prayer to Mary after Holy Communion

O VIRGIN Mother of Jesus, you received Him through the Holy Spirit with the greatest respect and love. Prompt all who receive the same Lord and Savior in Holy Communion to express their love and gratitude to Him. Help them resolve to spend the day in loving union with Jesus, with the Father, and with the Spirit of Holiness Who is Your beloved Spouse. Amen.

11. Prayer with the Church

MERCIFUL Father, Your Son Jesus Christ sent the Holy Spirit from You, as His first *gift* to those who believe, to complete His work on earth and bring us the fullness of grace.

Father, Most Holy One, all holiness comes from You through Your Son Jesus and by the working of the Holy Spirit. Make us learn to imitate Your Son and *follow* the inspirations of the *Holy Spirit*. Amen.

12. Prayer for Overcoming the Enemy

HOLY Spirit, You led Jesus into the desert where He overcame Satan, the arch-deceiver. Grant to faithful Catholics the means to overcome the evil forces that are presently inspiring disunity in the Church in matters of essential beliefs and fundamental laws of moral conduct.

Saint Michael the Archangel, defend us in the battle. Be our protection against the malice and the snares of the devil. We humbly beseech God to restrain him, and may you, Prince of the heavenly army, by the power of God cast into hell Satan and the other evil spirits who roam through the world seeking the ruin of souls. Amen.

13. Litany of the Holy Spirit
For Private Devotion

THE word "litany" comes from a Greek word that means prayer. Short invocations to which the assembly answered during processions were called litanies. Here we give a Litany of the Holy Spirit.

LORD, have mercy. *Christ have mercy.* Lord, have mercy.

Holy Spirit, hear us. *Holy Spirit, graciously hear us.*

God, the Father of heaven, *have mercy on us.*

God, the Son, Redeemer of the world, *have mercy on us.*

God, the Holy Spirit, *have mercy on us*

Holy Trinity, one God . . .

Holy Spirit, Who proceed from the Father,

Holy Spirit, co-equal with the Father and the Son,

Promise of the Father, most bounteous,

Gift of God Most High,

Ray of Heavenly Light,

Author of all good,

Source of Living Water,

Consuming Fire,

Burning Love,

Spiritual Unction,

Spirit of Truth and Power,

Spirit of Wisdom and Understanding,
Spirit of Counsel and Fortitude,
Spirit of Knowledge and Piety,
Spirit of Fear of the Lord,
Spirit of Compunction,
Spirit of Grace and Prayer,
Spirit of Charity, Peace, and Joy,
Spirit of Patience,
Spirit of Longanimity and Goodness,
Spirit of Benignity and Mildness,
Spirit of Fidelity,
Spirit of Modesty and Continence,
Spirit of Chastity,
Spirit of Adoption of children of God,
Holy Spirit, Comforter,
Holy Spirit, Sanctifier,
You through Whom spoke holy men of God,
You Who overshadowed Mary,
You by Whom Mary conceived Christ,
You Who descend upon humans at Baptism,
You Who, on the Day of Pentecost, appeared
    through fiery tongues,
You by Whom we are reborn,
You Who dwell in us as in a Temple,
You Who govern and animate the Church,
You Who fill the whole world,
That You may renew the face of the earth,
                we beseech You, hear us.

That You may shed Your Light upon us,
we beseech You, hear us.
That You may pour Your Love into our hearts,
That You may inspire us to love our neighbor,
That You may teach us to ask for the graces
we need,
That You may enlighten us with Your heavenly inspirations,
That You may guide us in the way of holiness,
That You may make us obedient to Your
commandments,
That You may teach us how to pray,
That You may always pray with us,
That You may inspire us with horror for sin,
That You may direct us in the practice of
virtue,
That You may make us persevere in a holy
life,
That You may make us faithful to our vocation,
That You may grant us good priests and Bishops,
That You may give us good Christian families,
That You may grant us a spiritual renewal of
the Church,
That You may guide and console the Holy
Father,
Lamb of God, Who take away the sins of the
world, *spare us, O Lord.*

Lamb of God, Who take away the sins of the
world, *graciously hear us, O Lord.*

Lamb of God, Who take away the sins of the
world, *have mercy on us.*

Holy Spirit, hear us.
Holy Spirit, graciously hear us.
Lord, have mercy.
Christ, have mercy.
Lord, have mercy.
Create a clean heart in us.
Renew a right spirit in us.

Let us pray

O MERCIFUL Father, grant that Your Divine Spirit may cleanse, inflame, and
enlighten our minds and hearts.

Enable us thereby to be fruitful in good
works for the glory of Your Majesty and for
the spiritual and material well-being of
human beings. We ask this through Jesus
Christ Your Son and the Holy Spirit. Amen.

14. Prayer to the Trinity for Priestly Vocations

M ERCIFUL *Father,* Your Son taught us to
pray for Your glory, that Your will might
be done; and also for our needs of both body
and soul, that we might overcome the Evil
One.

According to Your design, priests must lead people to honor You in the Holy Sacrifice of the Mass. They must nourish them with the True Bread from Heaven. They must help them to be reconciled with You, teach them to observe Your Commandments, and aid them to grow in holiness during their pilgrimage upon earth.

Grant us holy, zealous priests, true spiritual fathers, of whom the Church today is in so great a need. *Dear Jesus Christ,* when You became man You, at the same time, were *anointed* as High Priest. Later on You chose to become also a *victim* of sacrifice, atoning for our sins.

You told us explicitly to pray that the Lord of the harvest might send laborers into His field.

Have compassion on Mother Church who does not have a sufficient number of priests. Send us men who are other Christs, who will zealously continue Your sanctifying work.

Dear Holy Spirit, by Whom Christ the Anointed Priest was conceived in Mary, inspire many men with the desire to serve God and others in the Christian Priesthood. Inspire parents with the desire to bring up obedient, prayerful children from among whom some may be led to embrace the Priestly Vocation.

Chapter 8

THE SUPERNATURAL LIFE AND THE HOLY SPIRIT

Supernatural Life

Follower:

DIVINE Sanctifier, I should like to talk with You about the Supernatural Life. We have been told that through Baptism of water and the Holy Spirit we are *born again,* born to a higher kind of life, a supernatural life that lasts eternally. We were told that it consists of participating in the intimate life of the Three Divine Persons, of the Holy Trinity.

Of course, we remain human but God wants us to belong also to His *family* as adopted children. We are told that this is not make-believe, as when, on earth, a child is legally adopted by a family. It is sometimes very painful for a child legally adopted to find out that this "father" and this "mother" are not truly his or her parents.

Holy Spirit:

That is very true. Recall what St. John tells you in his Gospel: *Any who did accept Him*

*He empowered to become children of God . . .
who were begotten . . . by God* (Jn 1:12-13).
And in his First Epistle he joyfully writes: *See
what great love the Father has bestowed on us,
enabling us to be called the children of God,
and that is what we are* (1 Jn 3:1-2).

Recall also that Jesus brought out how intimate the life of Divinely adopted children is
with Father, Son, and Holy Spirit. Jesus said:
"*Abide in Me as I abide in you. . . . I am the
vine, you are the branches. Whoever abides in
Me, and I in him, will bear much fruit* (Jn
15:4-5).

St. Paul brings out well the family relationship with God: *You [received] . . . the
Spirit of adoption, enabling us to cry out,
"Abba! Father!" The Spirit Himself bears witness with our spirit that we are children of
God. And if we are children, then we are heirs
—heirs of God and joint heirs with Christ,
provided that we share His sufferings so that
we may also share His glory* (Rom 8:15-17).

This then is "supernatural life" as you are
accustomed to call it.

You know also what St. Paul says about that
in another Epistle: *And to offer proof that you
are children, God has sent into our hearts the
Spirit of His Son, crying out "Abba! Father!"*

Therefore, you are no longer a slave but a child; and if you are a child, then you are also an heir by the will of God (Gal 4:6-7).

Human beings in a certain sense are slaves of God because God has created them and therefore is an absolute owner of them. But God treats you instead as friends, even as children, and wants humans to be with the Divine Trinity for all eternity as most beloved adopted children, giving them a share in His Divine Nature. This brings out how greatly God loves people.

To each one of the Three Divine Persons, as you have stated, a particular role belongs within the Trinity. And to each one of the Divine Persons, for that reason and for others also, a special role is attributed in relation to human beings.

Role of the Holy Spirit in Our Supernatural Life

Follower:

IN THE Creed that we recite on Sundays at Mass (Council of Nicea, 325, and of Constantinople, 381) we profess a most consoling truth: "We believe in the Holy Spirit, the Lord, the Giver of life, Who proceeds from the Father and the Son. With the Fa-

**THE TRINITY IS CLOSELY RELATED TO OUR SAL-
VATION** — Jesus told His disciples: "Go, therefore,
and make disciples of all nations, baptizing them in
the Name of the Father and of the Son and of the Holy
Spirit" (Mt 28:19).

ther and the Son He is worshiped and glorified. He has spoken through the Prophets."

You, Holy Spirit, give us *supernatural life*.
This is above our nature and thus, of course,
above our understanding. I like the Gospel of
St. John, the disciple whom Jesus loved. How
well he brings out what Jesus said to
Nicodemus who lived still very much on the
purely natural level and could not imagine
how anyone could be "born again."

Jesus said: *"Amen, amen, I say to you, no
one can see the Kingdom of God without being
born from above. . . . Amen, amen, I say to you,
no one can enter the Kingdom of God without
being born of water and the Spirit. . . . So it is
with everyone who is born of the Spirit"* (Jn 3:3-
5, 8).

The Life of the Spirit in Reborn People

Holy Spirit:

GOD alone—Father, Son, and Holy Spirit
—lives "from" all eternity. In God there
is no change, no time. When human beings
speak of being begotten, or of proceeding
from someone, they imply change and time.
In God, "generation" and "proceeding
from" imply no succession of any kind.
Humans cannot understand such things.

Neither can they understand how God can make humans have a share in Divine life. If someone is faithful, as St. Paul was from his conversion to the end of his life, he can say with the Apostle: *And now it is no longer I who live, but it is Christ Who lives in me* (Gal 2:20).

When you have dispositions similar to those of that great convert, you then have the thoughts, the affections, the desires, the volitions of Jesus. You then tend to humble yourself in imitation of the Son of God.

Choosing to become the Son of Man, He as it were annihilated Himself, taking the form of a servant, of a slave. Having become the son of Mary, He was animated by Me. In all circumstances He let Himself be moved by Me. So must reborn persons let themselves be "guided by the Holy Spirit."

St. Paul speaks bluntly when he tells you: *Anyone who does not possess the Spirit of Christ cannot belong to Him.* But he adds: *All those who are led by the Spirit of God are children of God* (Rom 8:9, 14).

Follower:

Our theologians try to express these sublime things but cannot help using inadequate human words. As you know, they tell us that supernatural life, or sanctifying grace, is essentially a participation in the filiation of the Word (of the Second Person), which filiation the Heavenly Father produces in us through the Divine Spirit, raising us rational creatures to the level of something Divine.

We can therefore say with St. Peter that the supernatural life is also a participation in the Divine Nature. Of course, this does not mean we cease to be creatures and "become God"! But one thing we believe, that through You, Holy Spirit, we are regenerated, we are raised and elevated in a way that we mortals are unable to understand and appreciate.

Basing themselves on Holy Scripture and the teaching of the Church's Magisterium, theologians tell us that we receive the *infused* virtues of Faith, Hope, and Charity, as well as the *moral virtues* (sometimes called *cardinal* virtues) of Prudence, Justice, Fortitude, and Temperance. These, they tell us, enable our faculties to act in a supernatural way, which disposes us for eternal life in heaven.

Holy Spirit:

It is more important to be blest with all these gratuitous Gifts than to know how to define them exactly. It is useful, however, to let people know "The Gifts of the Holy Spirit," for knowledge of values leads to desire for them.

These gifts enable your faculties to receive the Divine cooperation, the supernatural help you call "actual grace." At times, such a help is indispensable in order that your faculties may act effectively on the supernatural level.

Follower:

Dear Holy Spirit, I am glad that we need not have a complete understanding of those "heavenly realities," and we know that You work in us most frequently unperceived in perfect silence.

Something for which all of us who are reborn through You must be grateful is God's infinite goodness in enabling us to live in a most intimate union with the Three Divine Persons so that we truly share in the Trinitarian Life.

If we could only realize ever more the unbelievable gift of God that St. Paul reveals when he exclaims: *The love of God has been poured into our hearts through the Holy Spirit Who has been given to us* (Rom 5:5).

God, Giver of Heavenly Gifts

Holy Spirit:

IT CAN never be sufficiently emphasized that God is Infinite Goodness. You know that goodness wants to diffuse itself. God is Infinite Goodwill. You call God Lord. He is —but not in the manner of human lords who can be tyrants and slave-drivers, seeking only their own pleasure.

God stands revealed as a most merciful Father and a most loving Shepherd. The Psalms, which you received from men who lived under the Old Dispensation, prompt you to say and sing: *I will sing forever of the Lord's kindness* (Ps 89:2).

God is supremely a Giver. So greatly did He love human beings that He gave them His only Son as a Victim of sacrifice for their sins, as a Savior Who enabled them to be adopted children of God.

Follower:

The trouble with us, Holy Spirit, is that we read, hear, and say these things so often that they become routine expressions. How greatly we need You—to open the eyes of our minds to those wonderful truths, those most precious facts.

We sometimes say: *How can I repay the Lord for all the good He has done for me?* (Ps 116:12). Innumerable are the things we have received, but how easily we forget or neglect to give thanks. Besides our existence as human beings, we have received sanctifying and actual graces. How very often we have received Jesus our Lord and Savior in Holy Communion, the Sacrament of Reconciliation, instruction regarding what we must believe and what we are expected to do and to avoid.

Yes indeed: *How shall I make a return to the Lord for all the good He has done for me?* Holy Spirit, Goodwill of Father and Son, grant us the gift of *gratitude* that expresses itself not in mere nice words but in truly *following You, Holy Spirit*, in all our thoughts, words, and actions.

The Holy Spirit Acts in Our Souls

Follower:

HOW greatly I desire to understand better Your action in the souls of people not in order to have knowledge of that privilege but in order to be animated by You in all I do.

I know that in the natural order we are influenced constantly by countless visible, and also very many invisible, things. We are influenced by parents, teachers, books, newspapers, television, radio, and by many things present in the atmosphere.

More powerful and always more beneficial is Your constant action in us, Holy Spirit, Host as well as Guest of our souls.

Follower:

Once again, Divine Spirit, how necessary it is for us to have a practical faith in what we have been taught: that the Holy Spirit moves, impels, instigates us by His Divine inspirations and impulses which we call "actual graces."

We learned that, ordinarily, if we want the Holy Spirit to act in us, we must be in the state of sanctifying grace. We learned about "Infused Virtues" about "Gifts of the Holy Spirit" which dispose us to act in a supernatural way. But is it not true that for a good number of Christians these are dead letter words?

Dear Holy Spirit, could we now speak a little about the *Infused Virtues.*

Holy Spirit:

An atheist *believes* many things, such as news broadcasts. He *hopes* to have success, good weather. He can *love* and be *charitable.* However, all this can remain on the purely natural level. What you want to talk about is supernatural virtues.

A bulb will not give light by itself. It depends on electricity. A motor will not start and continue to function without the particular fuel that suits it.

Similarly, in order that you may be able to act in a supernatural way you need the supernatural virtues. No doubt you learned that Faith, Hope, and Charity are names given to such virtues. And here we are not speaking of natural faith, hope, and charity.

By supernatural Faith, as you say in your "Acts," You firmly believe all the truths that God has revealed. And you add "because You [God] have revealed them Who can neither deceive nor be deceived."

By supernatural Hope you expect, with absolute confidence in the Divine Goodness, eternal life and the helps that are necessary to attain it.

By supernatural Charity (Love) you are enabled to love God above all things, and love your neighbor as yourself out of love for God.

When an act of perfect love of God is joined to contrition for your sins. such a perfect act of contrition could be called an *insurance for eternal life.*

Pray often for an increase in those supernatural virtues. They will powerfully help you
in your progress in holiness, your progress in
the *way of perfection.*

Follower:

Why do theologians specially connect You
with those Infused Virtues?

Holy Spirit:

As you realize, to be Christ-centered or
God-the-Father-centered does not detract
from Me. Most Church prayers are addressed
to the Father. It is natural to pay special attention to the Son because He became like
men in all things except sin. With respect to
the infused virtues of Faith, Hope, and Charity that are all God-centered, it is not difficult
to see why a special reference is made to
Me.

Recall Luke's report regarding what was
effected through My "coming" at Pentecost.
Mary who prayed with the Apostles before
Pentecost had already shown her faith when
I overshadowed her at the Annunciation and
when Elizabeth said to her at the Visitation:
"Blessed is she who believed" (Lk 1:45). Mary
certainly trusted fully in the fulfillment of
God's promises. And it is perfectly clear that

THE HOLY SPIRIT COMES UPON MARY—"The Angel answered [Mary], 'The Holy Spirit will come upon you, and the power of the Most High will overshadow you.' . . . Mary said, 'Behold, I am the servant of the Lord. Let it be done to me according to your word' " (Lk 1:35, 38).

Mary who is called My Spouse was full of love
that I had poured into her heart a long time
before Pentecost.

The change in the Apostles regarding faith,
hope, and love through My coming at Pentecost is well known.

A good number of those who had witnessed
the strange happenings—a mighty wind,
flames of fire, speaking in tongues—believed
and hoped in salvation and learned to be charitable, becoming *one in heart and mind*. So
they were baptized, and at the same time that
they received the grace of being supernaturally
reborn, they received the infused virtues of
Faith, Hope, and Charity.

Follower:

Holy Spirit, permit me to recite:

Archconfraternity Prayer to the Holy Spirit

HOLY Spirit, Lord of Light,
From Your clear celestial height,
Your pure beaming radiance give.
Come, O Father of the Poor,
Come with treasures that endure,
Come, O Light of all that live.
You of all Consolers best,
And the soul's delightsome Guest,

Do refreshing Peace bestow.
You in toil are Comfort sweet,
Pleasant Coolness in the heat,
Solace in the midst of woe.
Light immortal, Light Divine,
Visit now this heart of mine,
And my inmost being fill.
If You take Your grace away,
Nothing pure in us will stay,
All our good is turned to ill.
Heal our wounds, our strength renew,
On our dryness pour Your Dew,
Wash the stains of guilt away.
Bend the stubborn heart and will,
Melt the frozen, warm the chill,
Guide the steps that go astray.
On all those who evermore
You confess and You adore,
In Your *Sevenfold Gifts* descend.
Give them *Comfort* when they die.
Give them Life with You on high,
Give them Joys that never end. Amen.

Dear Holy Spirit, what a pity that we do not more frequently ponder such fundamental and most consoling words. They most powerfully show us the great value of Your manifold activity in people's souls.

Chapter 9

THE GIFTS OF THE HOLY SPIRIT

Holy Spirit:

ST. LUKE tells you that Jesus, (after His stay in the desert), *filled with the power of the Spirit, returned to Galilee.* He then chose to read the following passage from Isaiah: *The Spirit of the Lord is upon Me, because He has anointed Me to bring the Good News to the poor* (Lk 4:14, 18).

When you read Isaiah at that place you learn that *a shoot will spring forth from the stump of Jesse [father of David], and a branch will grow from his roots. The Spirit of the Lord will rest upon Him: a Spirit of wisdom and understanding, a Spirit of counsel and power, a Spirit of knowledge and fear of the Lord [piety], and His delight will be the fear of the Lord* (Isa 11:1-12).

After the reading, Jesus added: *"Today this Scripture has been fulfilled in your presence"* (Lk 4:21). Here, once more, Luke witnesses to Christ and to Me, Whom you call Holy Spirit.

Here once more you realize how difficult it is for human language properly to express supernatural realities. Your words first refer to natural not supernatural things. There are many kinds of wisdom, knowledge, understanding, fear. There is, for instance, purely human wisdom like that of the Greek philosophers.

When prayers are recited that use such terms, it is important to explain from time to time what they mean in the context of "gifts of the Holy Spirit."

It has been well said that in persons who are wholly committed to God, the gifts of the Holy Spirit are like Divine "instincts." Think of Jesus and also of Mary. Many Saints tried to act and did act in all circumstances as Mary would have done.

Seven Great Gifts of the Holy Spirit

Follower:

I KNOW that wisdom is the supreme gift. It enables us to be wholly committed to You. It makes us relish God above all else and whatever is concerned with the glory of God. Those who act in virtue of this gift are said to be able to do or suffer everything for God's greater glory. It might be well to remind ourselves of this aspect of our lives from time to time. One way in which such a reminder was accomplished in the past was by the custom of writing at the top of letters or examination papers, etc.: A.M.D.G. which stood for the Latin words *Ad maiorem Dei gloriam:* "For the greater glory of God."

Holy Spirit:

The gift of *understanding* enables a person to penetrate in a wonderful way into a mystery of the Faith or into the meaning of words inspired by the Holy Spirit. Think of the supernatural understanding of uneducated persons like St. Bernadette of Lourdes who spread devotion to Mary and St. Margaret Mary of Paray Le Monial who spread devotion to the Sacred Heart.

Follower:

We have psychological counselors. I know that Your gift of *counsel* makes us discern as by instinct what has to be done in every circumstance, whether it concerns our own conduct or the conduct of others. A man who seems to have had the gift of counsel to a high degree was Venerable Francis Libermann, one of the greatest spiritual directors of the nineteenth century.

Yet he said: "We have only *one* Spiritual Director: the Holy Spirit. The role of a merely human spiritual director is to find out how You, the Counselor, guide a person, and then strive to help that person to recognize the Divine guidance and the obstacles that might be placed in the way.

As for the gift of *strength* (or *fortitude*), there seems little difficulty in understanding its meaning. It prompts us to undertake very difficult things and bear sufferings when this is in accord with God's will and is seen to be for God's glory. We have wonderful examples of fortitude not only in the martyrs who were swiftly put to death, but in those who suffered a prolonged martyrdom in sickness.

St. Paul must have suffered much in the second way although we do not know exactly what he meant by *the thorn in the flesh* (2 Cor 12:7) to which he alluded in passing. One thing St. Paul tells us that is fundamental: *[We] can do all things in Him Who strengthens [us]* (Phil 4:13). And You, dear Holy Spirit, help us with Your gift of fortitude!

Holy Spirit:

I am certain that the kind of "knowledge" in the gift of *knowledge* is not immediately understood by those who hear there is such a gift. There are many kinds of knowledge and many degrees of knowledge. Here you can understand by it the knowledge that enables you to judge things—for instance, events in this world, and particularly painful things—according to God's judgment about them.

How different is the judgment about persecution, illness, death, etc. on the part of a worldling and the judgment about such things on the part of a Saint. Perhaps this makes you recall the Beatitudes, which to some people seem to be insane statements.

Follower:

We have been told to avoid interpreting the gift of *piety* so as to mean a saccharine kind of "devotion." Some supposedly pious people make their piety consist in multiplying their prayers, as if quantity were better than quality, and sometimes they, at the same time, despise their neighbor and are proud about their "devotion."

True piety is like the "devotion" of a good child who shows great respect and love toward parents and lovingly obeys them. The gift of piety prompts a person to imitate the Heavenly Father, the Son and the Holy Spirit in their love for one another and in their love for their creatures made after their own image.

Holy Spirit:

There are many kinds of fear, for example, a criminal's fear of being detected, and the fear of a slave in relation to his tyrannical master. But fear as a gift of the Holy Spirit is wholly different; for a child of God knows God's infinite goodness and mercy, and what such a child fears more than anything else is offending the parents even in the least manner.

Think of St. Theresa of Lisieux, how she shunned even the slightest imperfection and was so sorry when she had failed somewhat in generosity. Did Teresa of Avila not promise to do always the better of two good things? And when she failed in the least way, how sorry she was! Worldlings would call this foolishness— but it is the foolishness of Saints!

So pray often for this gift of fear. The Little Flower was animated by a "spirit of child-hood," combining a holy kind of fear with a perfect confidence in the Infinitely Good God, to Whom she completely "*abandoned*" herself as children are often seen to abandon themselves to their mothers. "Unless you be-

come like little children. . . ." Often meditate
on this fundamental disposition.

Follower: 🧍

Thank You, dear Spirit of love, and let me
now pray for the seven gifts of the Holy Spirit.
As You see, in distinguishing *seven* gifts, I am
following what was accepted in the Vulgate
translation of the passage of Isaiah quoted
above (11:1-2) where the first occurrence of
the word *fear* in the original text was quali-
fied as piety.

Prayer for the Seven Gifts

HOLY Spirit, Sanctifier blest, deign to grant
us:

the gift of fear,
 which makes us shun all sin;
the gift of piety,
 which makes us respect and love
 the Three Divine Persons,
 our parents and children,
 as is proper for true children of God;
the gift of knowledge,
 which makes us judge eternal and temporal
  things
 as God judges them;
the gift of fortitude,
 which makes us bear all hardships
 for the love and greater glory of God;

the gift of counsel,
   which makes us be guided, and guide
      others,
   in the Way of Truth, of Christlike Life;
the gift of understanding,
   which makes us penetrate deeply into
   what You, Holy Spirit, have deigned to
      reveal;
the gift of wisdom,
   which makes us relish all that is right
   and is in line with Eternal Wisdom.
This we ask You to grant us,
   Gift of God Most High,
   Who live in perfect unity of Love
   with the Father and the Son. Amen.

Development of the Gifts

Follower: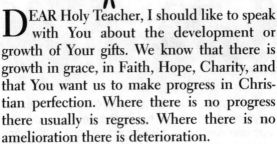

D EAR Holy Teacher, I should like to speak
with You about the development or
growth of Your gifts. We know that there is
growth in grace, in Faith, Hope, Charity, and
that You want us to make progress in Christian perfection. Where there is no progress
there usually is regress. Where there is no
amelioration there is deterioration.

We know the great means for making spiritual progress: Prayer, devout reception of the

JESUS GOES ABOUT DOING GOOD—"At sunset they brought to Him all those who were sick with various diseases. He laid His hands on each of them and healed them. . . . Thus He continued to preach [the Good News of the Kingdom of God]" (Lk 4:40-44).

Sacraments, reading Holy Scripture meditatively, helping others in imitation of Christ Who went about doing good.

Why is it that there are apparently so few Saints, that so many seem to fail to make spiritual progress?

Holy Spirit:

There are numerous and complex reasons. Today there is much ignorance about religious matters even among Catholics. And it is impossible to love, and love greatly, what is not known. But a major obstacle in the way of growth in holiness, in development of the gifts, is *pride*.

This is a very old sin. Recall that your first parents were told: *"When you eat [the forbidden fruit] . . . you will become like God"* (Gen 3:5). And they ate of it, proudly disobeying.

Pride, as you well know, lies at the root of many sins, for instance, disobedience to legitimate authority. "I will not serve" is a favorite motto of many human beings. That is one reason why Jesus Who was the eternal Son of God *emptied Himself, taking the form of a slave, . . . and became obedient to death* (Phil 2:7-8)—a most humiliating death after undergoing incredible insults. What more could the

Son of God, become Son of Man, have done to teach humility?

In spite of all that, even priests and religious, who took the vow of obedience, sometimes want to follow their own wills. In the home, too, there are youngsters who proclaim their independence from their parents, refusing to "honor father and mother," which is one of the great commandments.

Some theologians become so carried away with their learning that they reject what is explicitly taught by the Magisterium of the Church. They seem to forget Christ's warning: *"Whoever listens to you listens to Me, and whoever rejects you rejects Me"* (Lk 10:16).

The Son of God appeared as the obedient servant, and was able to say: *Learn from Me, for I am gentle and humble of Heart* (Mt 11:29).

Without God you can do *nothing*. Especially in the supernatural order, there will be no progress, no development of the precious gifts, if there is no Christlike humility.

You honor Mary and you rightly do so. You honor her principally by imitating her virtues, imitating the way she grew in the gifts of the Holy Spirit. She is a great example of humility.

When called to become My Spouse and the Mother of the Messiah, she called herself a servant of the Lord and obeyed without any reservation. After remaining in the background during Christ's public life, she reappeared standing near the Cross of shame, partaking of Christ's humiliation. God gives grace to the humble and enables them to develop the gifts of the Holy Spirit.

It is most useful, therefore, daily to examine your conscience and find out what words and actions were inspired by pride, and then to beg Me to help you overcome your pride and at the same time foster the growth of My gifts in you.

The Necessity of Humility

Follower:

WHEN we read the prayers of saintly men and women we cannot help wondering why they are so conscious of their "sinfulness," which makes them be so humble and even seek humiliations.

Holy Spirit:

The answer is not so difficult. Like St. Paul they could say: *I [will] know nothing except Jesus Christ—and Him crucified* (1 Cor 2:2), because of their constant meditation on the freely chosen self-humiliation of the glorious and eternal Son of God. This makes them realize the enormous difference between the Son of God Who "emptied" Himself, taking the form of a slave, and the greatest self-humiliation of a mere creature who is wholly dependent on God for all that he/she happens to have.

Follower:

How true, dear Holy Spirit. And I notice that, as saintly persons grow in holiness, they become ever more humble, for they realize that it is by the grace of God—and grace is gratuitous—that their greater perfection has been attained.

To worldlings some Saints might appear as psychologically disturbed, as sick persons.

In the fable, the peacock is pictured as proudly exhibiting his beautiful feathers. But peacocks are not able to sin by pride.

How very much we must all pray often and confidently to You, Holy Spirit, to make us realize that, as Venerable Francis Libermann expressed it, of ourselves we are *nothing* but God is all. How true also that our great book should be: *the inner life of Jesus and Mary*, which You, Holy Spirit, Divine Master, can make us understand ever better and love ever more.

Chapter 10

MORE PRAYERS TO RECEIVE
THE HOLY SPIRIT

Follower:

God Is All—Human Beings Are Nothing!

O MOST holy and adorable Spirit, make me listen to Your sweet and adorable voice. Before You, I want to be like a light feather, so that Your Breath may bring me where You want me to go, and in such obedience to You that I never place the smallest obstacle in Your way. This I ask You to grant me, for the greatest glory of the Heavenly Father, in Jesus Christ, our Lord, with Whom You live in perfect unity. Amen.

Maxims about Proper Spiritual Reading

READ the lives of the most fervent Saints. Read few spiritual authors. Read only a little of them at a time.

Our reading should be more for the heart than for the mind.

Our reading should be to make us fervent rather than learned.

Our great book should be the inner life of Jesus and Mary, written not by the hand of humans but by the hand of God Himself.

Our great Master, the Holy Spirit, speaks to us in the depths of our soul. Let us listen to Him. Let us be faithful to Him. He will sanctify us.   Venerable Francis Libermann

Grant Us the Good Spirit

HEAVENLY Father, refusing to rely on my righteousness, but putting all my confidence only in the promise of Your Only Son Who said: ". . . *How much more will the heavenly Father give the Holy Spirit to those who ask Him*" (Lk 11:13), I now send up this prayer to You.

Your Son is Truth itself. He does not deceive us. Fulfill, therefore, the promise Your Son made when He glorified You while on earth. He was obedient even unto death, the death of the Cross.

Give the Holy Spirit to those who ask You to give Him to them. Give me the spirit of fear and the spirit of love, that Your servant may fear nothing except offending You, and that I may love You alone and love my neighbor in You. Amen.   St. Robert Bellarmine

Holy Spirit, Purify My Soul

I HAVE prayed insistently, asking that my heart might become the tabernacle of the Holy Spirit. I have realized, however, how unclean I am in comparison with the Divine Spirit Who is so pure, Who is infinite Holiness and Love. I accept all sufferings and sorrows that the Holy Spirit may wish to have me undergo to make me pure.

Today, in Your presence and that of Your Spouse, the Blessed Virgin Mary, full of grace, I accept all crosses, all trials interior or exterior, that the Holy Spirit considers necessary to purify me.

While fully aware of my great weakness I know that You, Who are Love itself, love human beings. I commend my soul to You; You are my power and my consolation. I know also that the Mother of mercy will help and protect me. So, my heart is full of confidence.

Pierre Picot de Cloriviere (d. 1820)

Prayer Before a Crucifix

MOST kind and gentle Jesus, I cast myself upon my knees before You. With a most fervent desire I beg You to impress upon my heart and mind great Faith, Hope, and Love, together with profound sorrow for my sins while I contemplate Your infinite Charity and Mercy expressed in Your five wounds, and recall David's prophetic words: *They have pierced My hands and My feet. I can count all My bones* (Ps 22:17-18). Amen.

Fundamental Petitions

DEAR Jesus, make me know myself and know You.

Let me desire and love You above all things.

Make me do all things out of love of God.

Teach me how to humble myself while glorifying You.

Make me accept everything You wish me to undergo.

Make me forsake myself and imitate You,

Following the Spirit of the Father and the Son.

Let me distrust myself but put my trust in You.

Let me obey all lawful authority out of love of You.

Make me always keep my eyes on You

So that, guided by the Holy Spirit,

I may one day possess You eternally. Amen.

(St. Augustine)

Sulpician Prayer to Jesus

O JESUS, living in Mary,
Come and live in Your servants:

In the spirit of Your holiness,

In the fullness of Your power,

In the perfection of Your ways,

In the truth of Your mysteries.

Reign in us over all adverse powers

By Your Holy Spirit,

And for the glory of the Father. Amen.

Chapter 11

THE FRUITS OF THE HOLY SPIRIT

Follower:

DEAR Divine Teacher, I feel quite certain that if I were to talk to a group of people about the Fruits of the Holy Spirit a good number of my hearers would wonder what exactly I meant by such fruits. They know of course that our Lord said: *"You will know them by their fruits"* (Mt 7:20) and that He spoke of the necessity of bringing forth fruits of good works (Lk 3:8-9). But why speak here of fruits of the Holy Spirit?

When we consult theologians and Holy Scripture we learn that what is meant is: *the Christian virtues that have reached their perfect development.*

We are told also that, besides such *virtues,* there are *actions* as well as *states* of sanctity.

Here we must once more go back to what we find in the famous text of Isaiah (11:2) where we read: *A shoot will spring forth from the stump of Jesse, and a branch will grow from his roots. The Spirit of the Lord will rest upon Him.*

After that, when we consult St. Paul in his Epistle to the Galatians (5:22)—in its Vulgate translation—we find *twelve* fruits of the Holy Spirit: "Love, Joy, Peace; Patience and Longanimity; Goodness, Benignity, Mildness, Fidelity; (finally) Modesty, Continence, and Chastity.

All of these can be *summed up* in love of God and love of neighbor.

When we ask why there are just twelve, St. Thomas Aquinas is ready with an answer: "This is merely a symbolic number." When we look at fruit trees, what gives us particular admiration and pleasure is seeing "gorgeous" fruits. So, we are told, the fruits of the Holy Spirit are those that have reached a *high degree of perfection.*

Holy Spirit:

You do well to bring out that not all acts of virtue are called fruits of the Holy Spirit but only those that have a *high* quality. Here now are a few examples:

1) *LOVE (CHARITY)* means the fruit found in those who are wholly committed and entirely delivered to the Holy Spirit's action. It consists in *perfect* love of God and neighbor.

2) *JOY* means the *intense* and intimate satisfaction persons experience when they realize they are in possession of their Sovereign Good. They realize they are infinitely loved by the God of Love and in turn they love God with all the power of their free will.

3) *PEACE* is the quiet, *perfect* repose persons experience when they are wholly and perfectly submissive to the Divine Will.

4) *PATIENCE* means lovingly and *fully* accepting the trials that the Divine Goodness sees fit to let persons undergo.

5) *LONGANIMITY* consists in knowing how to wait, *feeling certain*, during trials, that God's moment will come, when He will fully aid sufferers.

6) *GOODNESS* here means truly desiring the good of *all* our brothers and sisters in Christ and also that of *all* our friends and our enemies, making no exception of any kind. This is the love of *perfect goodwill*.

Follower:

Dear Holy Spirit, this makes me think of Father Richard Whitford, who in the time of Henry VIII made a complete translation of *The Imitation of Christ* into English and who looked upon the Holy Spirit as being the

Goodwill between the Father and the Son, in the Holy Trinity.

You, Divine Spirit, animated many on the first Pentecost with such *goodwill*, so that the people marveled at their love for one another and their union of minds and hearts (Acts 2: 42-47).

Holy Spirit:

7) *BENIGNITY* means to procure for your brothers and sisters in Christ, without any distinction of persons, *all the good* you are able to give them. It is the love of *beneficence*.

8) *MILDNESS* means bearing with gentleness and patience all the defects of others, without ever yielding to improper anger. It is lovingly accepting—*always*—such troublesome things.

9) *FIDELITY* means *eagerly* rendering to all people all that you owe them. It is the *perfect* virtue of *justice*.

10) *MODESTY* means *always* and in every circumstance keeping the just and *golden mean*, the proper measure, and never falling into contrary excesses.

11) *CONTINENCE* means *fully* controlling the disorderly movements of one's sensible nature, in particular the movements con-

trary to perfect chastity. This then is the *laborious* chastity of the soul that suffers such temptations.

12) *CHASTITY* means perfect and *unalterable purity* when God, in His mercy, wants to preserve persons even from temptations against the virtue of *chastity*. Such, certainly, was the chastity of Jesus and Mary.

Follower:

Dear Sanctifier Blest, what You have explained shows most clearly that we are called to aim high, though never by relying on ourselves. There are unfortunately people who say: I am not a Saint, and who virtually add: I do not expect to become a Saint; I am satisfied with mediocrity. They seem never to have read or heard Christ's words: "*Strive to be perfect, just as your heavenly Father is perfect*" (Mt 5:48).

To all, sufficient grace is given to attain what God from all eternity expected of them. What a pity that many, while perhaps striving for perfection in a particular art or occupation, do not make use of the many means put at their disposal for *growth in holiness*, for producing precious fruits in accord with God's desire and with the help You, Holy Prompter and Guide, are always ready to give.

Prayer for the Twelve Fruits of the Spirit

H OLY Spirit, eternal Love of the Father and the Son, kindly bestow on us the fruit of *charity*, that we may be united to you by Divine Love; the fruit of *joy*, that we may be filled with holy consolation; the fruit of *peace*, that we may enjoy tranquility of soul; and the fruit of *patience*, that we may endure humbly everything that may be opposed to our own desires.

Divine Spirit, be pleased to infuse in us the fruit of *longanimity*, that we may not be discouraged by delay but may persevere in prayer; the fruit of *goodness*, that we may be benevolent toward all; the fruit of *benignity*, that we may willingly relieve our neighbor's necessities; and the fruit of *mildness*, that we may subdue every rising of ill temper, stifle every murmur, and repress the susceptibilities of our nature in all our dealings with our neighbor.

Creator Spirit, graciously impart to us the fruit of *fidelity*, that we may rely with assured confidence on the Word of God; the fruit of *modesty*, that we may order our exterior regularly; and the fruits of *continence* and *chastity*, that we may keep our bodies in such holiness as befits Your temple, so that having by Your assistance preserved our hearts pure on earth, we may merit in Jesus Christ, according to the words of the Gospel, to see God eternally in the glory of His Kingdom.

Chapter 12

DEVOTION TO THE HOLY SPIRIT

Follower:

DEAR Holy Spirit, you must pardon me for talking so much, but as you know Jesus urged us to be like little children and children normally deluge their parents with questions. What gives me confidence is that prayer is a *familiar* conversation with God Who, we know, loves us.

Furthermore, what I say to You is incorporated in a book in which the readers are invited to *follow* You, to put no obstacles in the way of Your wonderful guidance. So, permit me to express what I have learned about the special *devotion* or *cult* that we owe You. And if I say something foolish or incorrect, please tell me.

The word "devotion" as here used means devotedness. St. Philip Neri says that it is an act of the will by which we spontaneously, wholeheartedly, and joyfully offer ourselves to God, determined to do everything in our power for the greater glory of God.

It is easy to see that we owe this kind of "devotion" or devotedness to God: to the Father, to the Son and to You, Holy Spirit.

You act with and in us, and true devotion to You certainly must prevent us from counteracting You in Your sanctifying activity in us. But this is not enough. We must also invoke You and with Your help dispose ourselves to be moved, led, and inspired by You in all circumstances.

Holy Spirit:

That is true. When you act in such a way you are true followers of the Holy Spirit.

St. Paul, speaking in a very human way tells you not to *sadden the Holy Spirit* (Eph 4:30) nor to *quench* Me, that is, My action in you (1 Thes 5:19).

Follower:

We know that we, as it were, "quench" You when we commit a grievous sin. We "sadden" You when we commit a venial sin. There are those who say: "This is *only* a venial sin, only a small fault." However, a slight *fault* remains a fault, a slight impoliteness truly willed remains an *impoliteness.*

Please tell me, Holy Spirit, how I can become a better follower of You.

Holy Spirit:

With the help of the grace that I am always ready to give, you can always be properly disposed to follow Me. This is fundamental.

a) Often recall the basic fact that I am truly present in you, that I, truly, infinitely, love you with a merciful love, a love that is identical with the love with which the Father and the Son love you.

b) You must abandon yourself to Me without reservation so that I may accomplish in you all the designs of the Heavenly Father. At the same time, you must constantly beg Me to take possession of your whole being, of all your faculties, so that it can be truly said that, like Jesus and Mary, you no longer act any more at any time except through My holy inspiration.

c) Finally—and this will not be difficult—you must recognize your wretchedness and your weakness. Keeping that in mind, you must apply yourself to being faithful even in the smallest things, *moved by love* (the Love I pour into your heart).

Follower:

Pardon me, Holy Spirit. You certainly propose a high ideal! At the same time, it is foolish on my part to say that You propose the impossible. All things that God wants, I must repeat to myself, are possible for us, if we have a proper recourse to God, to You.

I must constantly repeat to myself: What more could God have done for me? What more could Jesus have done for me? What more can You do, dear Guest and Host, in my soul? How right St. Paul is in saying: "*I can do all things in Him Who strengthens me*" (Phil 4:13). And You are given to us by the Father and the Son, and come to our assistance with Divine and infinite power.

Thank You, Guide of my soul, for showing us the essentials regarding devotion to You. We know also that "consecrating" ourselves in a special way to You in no way detracts from what we owe to the other Divine Persons.

In virtue of Baptism we were already consecrated to the Most Holy Trinity. But it is most useful for us to repeat that consecration from time to time, especially because most of us were consecrated in Baptism when we were still too young to offer that consecration personally.

It is well for us to remember that You, Holy Spirit, are the Spirit of the Father and of the Son. It would be impossible for You to lead us away from either the Father or the Son. We have the wonderful privilege of being children of the Father, brothers and sis-

ters of the Son, and temples of You, Holy
Spirit.

St. Paul who was such a devoted follower of
Jesus Christ had at the same time a great devotion toward You, as is seen clearly when he tells
us: *All those who are led by the Spirit of God
are children of God* (Rom 8:14). St. Paul says to
all of us: *Be imitators of me, as I am of Christ*
(1 Cor 11:1). He could have said, similarly: Be
followers of the Holy Spirit, as I am.

Holy Spirit:

Here I wish to add once more: Devotion
must be devotedness. You should not be content with sweet sentiments of "devotion," as
are sometimes experienced for a short time by
novices. Christians, as followers of Jesus and of
Me, must aim at something higher than not
committing mortal sins, and higher than
merely avoiding venial sins.

They must aim at practicing the evangeli-
cal counsels. They must constantly remember
the words St. Luke records, referring to what
was already written in the Old Law: *You shall
love the Lord your God with all your heart, and
with all your soul, and with all your strength,
and with all your mind"* (Lk 10:27).

Chapter 13

THE BEATITUDES

Follower:

HOLY Teacher, Divine Spirit, You have told us to aim high, not out of ambition but for Your greater glory. And it seems that You may wish to explain to us the importance of the *Beatitudes* mentioned by Jesus Christ which, at the same time, promise us supreme happiness, which is well termed *"beatitude."*

Some look upon them as a kind of *constitution* or fundamental laws as well as ideals of the members of the Church, of the citizens of the Divine Kingdom.

All men naturally seek happiness, and our Lord in the so-called "Sermon on the Mount" mentions the reward when He urges us to strive for perfection. How very great that reward is already here in this life, but it is especially wonderful in the eternal life with God.

When we now consult Matthew (5:3-12) we count *eight* Beatitudes. And we notice that blessedness, great happiness, is promised to all who practice virtues in a high degree of perfection. We might even think of them as "fruits of the Holy Spirit." May I ask You to explain briefly the true meaning of some of them?

Holy Spirit:

The first one, in Matthew, reads: *Blessed are the poor in spirit.* It is clear, first of all, that there is no virtue in merely being poor. There are no poor people in heaven, and poor people on earth can be great lovers of earthly possessions, can even hate God and neighbor.

On the other hand, there are those like St. Francis of Assisi who are not only detached from earthly goods but have chosen to be actually poor regarding earthly possessions.

The rich young man, a good man who had "observed all the commandments" and asked Jesus what he was expected to do in order to be "perfect," was explicitly told by the Lord to get rid of his earthly possessions, to sell them and give the money to the poor! He proved to be a rich man who was not detached from such goods. Although explicitly called by the Lord in a very special way, he loved wealth more than following Christ in a special vocation.

A wealthy person can be detached from earthly goods, but such detachment is difficult. Hence, vows of poverty were introduced

JESUS PROCLAIMS THE BEATITUDES—"Then He began to teach [the crowds] as follows: 'Blessed are the poor in spirit, for theirs is the Kingdom of Heaven. Blessed are those who mourn, for they will be comforted. . . .' " (Mt 5:1-4).

and actual poverty was accepted by a good number of religious.

Those who have taken such vows, however, manage sometimes to get superfluous earthly goods at their disposal. Such religious are neither poor materially nor poor in spirit. This has made some say of them: "They *have* nothing, but in reality they *possess* everything!"

Christ, the Exemplar, chose to live in actual poverty. He had no home He called His own. He had chosen to be born of poor people in a stable, and He accepted death on a Cross despoiled of all earthly possessions. How powerful then is the example of the "poor man of Assisi," truly "another Christ" in his spirit of poverty and detachment!

Here then, as you said, is a veritable "fruit of the Holy Spirit": exercising a virtue *in a high degree of perfection.*

Follower:

The *second* is a rather strange Beatitude: *Blessed are those who mourn* [or *weep*]. May I ask You, Holy Spirit, to explain its true meaning?

Holy Spirit:

First of all, it is clear that there is no virtue in shedding tears. There are infants and even grown-ups who shed tears with the greatest facility and frequency. A robber might weep because he had failed to take anything.

Blessed truly are those who weep—even only spiritually—because they are sorry for having offended an infinitely good God; and Saints like Theresa of Lisieux could weep because they had failed to be generous in something of slight importance.

It can also mean: Blessed are those who are greatly afflicted but accept trials as Christ accepted them. Those persons try to accept sufferings in this spirit and look forward to heavenly life with God Who *will wipe every tear from their eyes* (Rev 21:4).

We have no particular difficulty in understanding the *third Beatitude: Blessed are the meek* [or *gentle*]. "Meekness" sometimes connotes something defective: spiritlessness. So we like to say about our dear Lord: He was *gentle and humble of heart.*

Follower:

The *fourth* Beatitude is: *Blessed are those who hunger and thirst for justice* [or *holiness*]. There was a Professor of Social Ethics who claimed that by this our Lord meant: Blessed are those who work for *social* justice. But, dear

Holy Spirit, You probably agree that this is not what Christ had in mind.

"Justice" here has a broader meaning. Human beings must first be just toward God and it is just and right always to thank, adore, love, and serve God. A godless communist can work hard for social justice while neglecting the all-important justice toward God, toward the Redeemer.

It seems to me that what Jesus taught us in the first part of the Our Father expresses our fundamental duty toward Him. We must hallow His Name, work for the coming of His Kingdom first in our hearts and in the hearts of others. We must always *try to do His will.*

Since the Beatitudes like the "Fruits of the Holy Spirit" refer to a high degree of perfection in practicing some virtues, we can say that this also means: Blessed are those who hunger for *perfection*, for *holiness*, as most generous *followers of the Holy Spirit.*

We find no difficulty regarding the meaning of the *fifth* Beatitude: *Blessed are the merciful.*

Such persons imitate the Heavenly Father Who is called the *"Father of Mercies"* (2 Cor 1:3). And we recite the words of the Psalmist: *I will sing forever of the Lord's kindness [mer-*

cies] (Ps 89:2). Of course, mere recitation or singing of such words is insufficient. Our Lord Jesus Christ has clear and strong words about that:

"But I say to you: Love your enemies and pray for those who persecute you. . . . If you love only those who love you, what reward will you receive? . . . Even the pagans do as much Therefore, strive to be perfect, just as your heavenly Father is perfect" (Mt 5:44-47). Our Father is infinitely merciful!

Holy Spirit:

You have done well recalling that fundamental point. Fr. Edward Leen, C.S.Sp., wrote well about Me. He said things worthwhile about the Beatitudes. Why not repeat for your readers what he said regarding the *sixth* Beatitude: *Blessed are the pure of heart?*

Follower:

First of all, Leen always tried to penetrate more deeply into the things God has deigned to reveal. He was a praying theologian and believed in *progress through mental prayer* (which served as the title for one of his books).

He considered this Beatitude to be fundamental and *all-embracing*. To be pure of heart, he explained, did not mean merely to be without sin, but to have an absolutely *pure intention*, the intention of truly and always doing and suffering *everything* for God's glory.

At the same time, those who have this Beatitude are wholly detached from everything that might lessen their attachment to God. For Leen, such purity of heart is as all-embracing as Charity, the Godlike Charity, a love *poured into our hearts through the Holy Spirit Who has been given to us* (Rom 5:5).

Holy Spirit:

We come now to the seventh Beatitude: *Blessed are the peacemakers* (Mt 5:9). Christ, we know, came as the Prince of Peace, of peace between human beings and God and peace among human beings. The Angels at Christ's *birth sang*: "*Glory to God in highest heaven, and on earth peace to all those on whom His favor rests*" (Lk 2:14).

Peace is the tranquility of order. There is perfect order and peace in heaven. What a sad thing—as history before the time of Christ and even after His coming reveals—that people, the so-called rational animals, *are war-mongers*.

You know the all-important lesson Jesus gave on the day of His glorious Resurrection when, appearing to His Apostles, He twice wished them peace and then said: *"Receive the Holy Spirit. If you forgive the sins of anyone, they are forgiven"* (Jn 20:19-23). This is the Sacrament of peace, of Reconciliation!

Jesus says to all of you: Follow My example. Be *peacemakers.*

Follower:

The eighth Beatitude is: *Blessed are those who are persecuted in the cause of justice* (Mt 5:10). How well the Christian martyrs, witnesses to Christ, have understood this throughout the ages. Inspired by You, Holy Spirit, they have come to their death rejoicing, because they were found worthy to follow the example of Jesus the greatest of martyrs, the greatest of those persecuted.

How well this privilege was appreciated by St. Paul who was persecuted and then murdered "for Christ's sake." He wrote: *Persecution will afflict all who want to lead a godly life in Christ* (2 Tim 3:12). Jesus added: *Blessed are you when you are forced to endure insults and cruel treatment and all kinds of calumnies for My sake.* Once more how silly such a statement seems to worldlings, to unbelievers.

Holy Spirit:

You rightly call all these Beatitudes, for they are *happiness-giving*. The rewards are expressed in various ways but the heavenly reward is: supreme and endless happiness. *Your reward will be great in heaven* (Mt 5:12).

One of the aspects of this reward is: *"They will see God"* (Mt 5:8). No one on earth can imagine or form an idea of what is called the Beatific Vision of God.

Follower:

O Holy Spirit, grant us to relish and to appreciate ever more the high ideals Jesus proposed to us. Already in this life those who, helped by You, aim at such perfection are the happiest of people. There are no sad Saints.

In contrast with them, how many are the reasons for sadness on the part of those whose god is something purely temporal.

How grateful we must be to You, O Holy Spirit, for revealing to us the way to *eternal, perfect happiness in heaven*. Amen.

Chapter 14

THE HOLY SPIRIT AND THE CHURCH

Follower:

I SHOULD like to talk with You about the Church, about divisions that exist not only among Christians but also among those who call themselves Catholics.

We know that You never meant to make the Bible that You inspired, the Bible privately interpreted, the sole guide regarding what we must believe, what we must do, and what we must avoid doing.

History shows that private interpretation of the Bible leads to division among Christians.

We Catholics possess the great safeguard of being guided by a Church Authority, the "Magisterium," which tells us the true meaning of texts of Holy Scripture, and tells us also what we must accept as having been transmitted by "Tradition."

We have been taught that the Church is the Society of those who, having received Baptism (of water and the Holy Spirit), profess one and same Faith under the guidance of the Pope (Vicar of Christ) and the Bishops who are in communion with the Pope.

We were also told that it is our Lord Jesus Christ Who, under the inspiration of the Holy Spirit, founded the "visible" Church upon earth.

Holy Spirit:

You know that Jesus Christ, Head of the Church, before His Passion, prayed for unity: *"[Father,] consecrate them in the truth. . . . I consecrate Myself, so that they too may be consecrated in truth. . . . I pray . . . also for those who through their word will come to believe in Me. May they all be one. As You, Father, are in Me and I in You, may they also be [one] in Us so that the world may believe that You have sent Me"* (Jn 17:17-21).

St. Paul emphasized the fact that there is a unity of the Church in virtue of the invisible Head, Jesus Christ, and also an invisible Soul Whom you call the Holy Spirit. Often meditate on what Paul says:

The body is a single unit, although it has many parts; and all . . . form one body. So it is with Christ. For in the one Spirit we were all baptized into one Body. . . . We were all given the same Spirit to drink (1 Cor 12:12-14).

St. Paul spoke with authority. He represented Christ and was animated by Me. Yet Paul

JESUS PRAYS FOR CHURCH UNITY—"I pray . . . also for those who through their word will come to believe in Me. May they all be one. As You, Father, are in Me and I in You, may they be [one] in Us" (Jn 17:20-21).

demanded obedience to those who had authority in the Church. Though especially called by God, he went to Jerusalem to see the Apostles (Acts 9:28) and to consult with Peter the "Rock" (Gal 1:18).

Follower:

Dear Holy Spirit, I hope and pray that *all* Catholics and *all Christians* may accept the Church as willed by God—one organized and ruled by visible authority. Empowered by grace, under Your inspiration, Holy Spirit, may all work for the growth of Christ's Mystical Body, the Church, in unity of belief, in unity of obedience, in unity of love, a love You pour into our hearts.

Holy Spirit:

You have recalled what Luke wrote about the First Pentecost when the Church founded by Christ was manifested in a spectacular way to the world. Accordingly, you speak of the "Birth of the Church," on that Pentecost.

In the Creed that you recite on Sundays you say emphatically: "We believe in One, Holy, Catholic, and Apostolic Church." These fundamentals should be well explained and insisted upon by preachers and teachers.

Follower:

Holy Spirit, we were taught that the *signs* that enable us to recognize the Visible Church, truly founded by Jesus Christ, were precisely these four "notes": unity, holiness, catholicity, and apostolicity.

We have been taught by the Church that Jesus brought the same Good News to all people and called them to the same new life. His Church is the union of those who follow His call. We know that Mother Church teaches *holiness* and has had many Saints throughout the ages. It does not mean of course that all her members are actually holy persons.

Catholicity we know means "for the whole world," universal. Popes and Bishops are successors of the Apostles, but all of us must cooperate in bringing the Good News, the sanctifying and saving grace to all people.

We can all exercise an *apostolate* of prayer and suffering, of setting the example of a true follower of Jesus, a true follower of the Holy Spirit.

We know that it is the *Roman* Catholic Church alone that possesses all the Signs and Notes of the True Church of Christ. She is the worldwide missionary and apostolic community of the followers of Jesus that is united around the Pope.

People often wonder how many will actually be saved. We know that God is infinitely merciful. He will not punish those who do all they can with the help of Your grace to do God's will. Only those who knowingly and voluntarily refuse to belong to the true Church of Christ will be condemned.

Dear Holy Spirit, could You once more tell us why we are justified in calling You the Soul of the Church, just as we call Jesus Christ the Head of the Church?

Holy Spirit:

You know that St. Augustine said: The Holy Spirit *does* in the Church what the soul *does* in the (human) body. So think of what the soul does in your body; it unifies and brings unity into the members of the body. It makes you be human, a rational being, in contrast with plants and beasts. It forms, organizes, and fosters growth. Lastly, it is the source of all the vital operations in the body.

The application is easy. The Holy Spirit is clearly the unifier. Unfortunately, there are Catholics who counteract Me by sowing dissension. You know that I am the Spirit of the

Father, and the Spirit of the Son. You can also say that I make you truly members of "God's Family." children of God.

Follower:

Yes, this reminds me of the wonderful words of St. Paul: *And to offer proof that you are children [of God], God has sent into our hearts the Spirit of His Son, crying out "Abba! Father!" Therefore, you are no longer a slave but a child; and if you are a child, then you are also an heir by the will of God* (Gal 4:6).

It is also clear that You, Holy Spirit, have presided over the formation of the Church and continue to watch over her life and growth: *It was in one Spirit that we were all baptized into one Body. . . . We were all given the same Spirit to drink* (1 Cor 12:13).

Prayer for the Church

IN UNION with the Praying Church we pray: Send forth Your Spirit and renew the world:

O God, in the beginning You created heaven and earth, and in the fullness of time You restored all things through Christ. Renew the world now through Your Holy Spirit.

You formed man and blew into him the Breath of life. Send now Your Spirit into the Church that she may give new life to mankind.

Enlighten all people by the Light of the Spirit and dispel the darkness of our time. Change hatred into love, sorrow into joy, warfare into peace.

You introduce people into life and glory, through the Holy Spirit. Grant to the deceased the joys of love in the Heavenly Kingdom.

You promised the Holy Spirit, that He might teach us all things and remind us of all that Your Son Jesus Christ has deigned to teach. Send us Your Spirit to strengthen our Faith, our Hope, and our Love.

This we ask, Heavenly Father, through Jesus Christ, Your Son Who lives with You in the unity of the Holy Spirit. Amen.

Chapter 15

THE MISSIONARY CHURCH

Follower:

POPE Paul VI wrote an inspiring *Apostolic Exhortation* in which he stressed the fact that the Church is *missionary*. When people hear the word "missionary," their first thought usually is that it points to those who go, who are "sent," to foreign countries to propagate the Faith. Hence, they must find it difficult to understand how the Church, as a whole, can be "missionary."

In the Creed we express the "notes" of the Church by saying that she is One, Holy, Catholic, and Apostolic. Surely, this does not mean that all the members of the Church are holy. Neither does it mean that all are "apostles" as were the first Twelve Apostles.

It is useful to try to understand words properly, especially when they point to things that are important. And this is the case when a Council and a Pope declare that the Church is missionary.

Holy Spirit:

Let Me recall for you that the Son of God and I Myself are rightly said to have had special "missions" in relation to human beings. You know well that the Eternal Son of God was sent, came for a special mission, for the work of evangelizing all human beings. He brought the Good News and He founded a Church of which He remains the invisible Head.

The successors of Peter, Vicar of Christ, and the Bishops, successors of the Apostles, must continue Christ's mission. They have the mission to continue the work of Christian evangelization until the end of time. It is clear, therefore, that the Church is missionary, first of all in those who govern the members of the Church, particularly in those who, in the Church, are the Magisterium" (Official Teachers).

Christ's Church has a sacred and supreme obligation of evangelizing mankind and can repeat with St. Paul: *The obligation to [preach the Gospel] has been given to me, and woe to me if I fail to fulfill it* (1 Cor 9:16). You know that Jesus, the Lord, gave the Church a mandate, a command, an order that all might believe and might be saved. It concerns the salvation of human beings made after the image of God.

The missionary Church is given a wisdom that is not of "this world." She is a divinely chosen instrument to arouse faith, a faith in divinely revealed *truth*. God IS Truth; and the "apostle," the "missionary," those who in a special way are appointed to continue Christ's work, should consecrate to it all their time and all their energy. If necessary, they should even be willing to sacrifice their life for that greatest of Causes.

Follower:

Here again, dear Holy Spirit, I cannot help recalling the wholly human and at the same time wholly Divine Evangelist Who virtually proclaimed this when, quoting Isaiah, He applied to Himself the words: *"The Spirit of the Lord is upon Me, because He has anointed Me to bring the Good News to the poor"* (Lk 4:18).

Jesus, the High Priest, was the first and the greatest Evangelist. He accomplished His mission perfectly even going so far as to sacrifice His earthly life in the process.

Today there is much talk about liberation. Sometimes it is greatly different from the kind

THE SPIRIT IS UPON JESUS—"He stood up to read,
. . . 'The Spirit of the Lord is upon Me, because He has
anointed Me to bring the Good News to the poor.' . . .
'Today this Scripture has been fulfilled in your presence' " (Lk 4:16-21).

of liberation that Christ brought and that the Church has the mandate to bring to people.

Holy Spirit:

It is a good thing to work for the liberation of people from any kind of oppression, to work for the true freedom that belongs to children of God. But it is necessary above all to liberate people from the slavery of sin and the slavery of Satan, to give them the joy of knowing that God loves people infinitely, the joy of loving God with all their heart.

People must come to know what is meant by the *Kingdom* or *Reign* of God and by salvation. These are fundamentals in evangelization, in the Good News.

All persons can receive that Kingdom and that salvation as a grace coming from God's infinite Mercy, but they should not be Quietists, remaining absolutely passive, doing absolutely nothing. *For just as the body is dead without a spirit, so faith without works is also dead* (Jas 2:26).

Jesus told you that everyone must, at the same time, attain that Kingdom through violence: *"The violent are taking it by force"* (Mt 11: 12). Members of the Church must accept fatigue and sufferings. They must practice self-abnegation and be willing to bear their cross, animated by the spirit of the Beatitudes.

Follower:

Yes, this is what we were taught. Our teachers spoke of *"metanoia,"* a total interior turnaround, a radical conversion, a profound change of outlook, a complete change of heart. We must all imitate Jesus Christ and His way of proclaiming the Kingdom of God. He accomplished it by His words and actions, by His signs and miracles, and most particularly by His voluntarily chosen Death, His Resurrection, and His sending of You, "the Spirit of truth" to us.

We Christians should be *enthusiastic.* This word, it seems, means God within *(En Theos).* Too few people are enthusiastic about God's design for us, about what Christ and You brought us: God within, God's Reign within, God's Salvation within, and—for those who remain faithful servants—Eternal Blessedness through union with God.

The Mission of the Church

Holy Spirit:

YOU were taught that the Church was born in virtue of the evangelization of Jesus. The "Church" in turn is sent by Him to evangelize the world: *"Go forth into every part of the world and proclaim the Gospel to all cre-*

ation. Whoever believes and is baptized will be saved; whoever does not believe will be condemned" (Mk 16:15-16).

There have been too many Christians who have not sufficiently realized that spreading the Gospel is not confined to the relatively few priests. It is true that Jesus gave His command to a handful of Apostles, but in a different way from what is imposed on priests, evangelization is also *the task of all Christians,* of all the members of the *Missionary* Church.

Recall what St. Peter told ordinary Christians, whom you call the faithful: *[You are] living stones, let yourselves be built up into a spiritual temple and become a holy priesthood to offer spiritual sacrifices acceptable to God through Jesus Christ* (1 Pet 2:5).

Also recall what the Second Vatican Council said on this matter under My inspiration:

"The whole Church is missionary, and the work of evangelization is a basic duty of the people of God. . . . As members of the living Christ, incorporated into Him . . . through Baptism, Confirmation, and the Eucharist, all the faithful are duty-bound to cooperate in the expansion and growth of His Body, to bring it to fullness as soon as may be" (*Decree on the Missionary Activity of the Church*, nos. 35-36).

"In the Church there is a diversity of ministry but a oneness of mission. Christ conferred on the Apostles and their successors the duty of teaching, sanctifying, and ruling in His Name and power. But the laity likewise share in the priestly, prophetic, and royal office of Christ and therefore have their own share in the mission of the whole People of God in the Church and in the world.

"They exercise the apostolate in fact by their activity directed to the evangelization and sanctification of human beings and to the penetrating and perfecting of the temporal order through the spirit of the Gospel" (*Decree on the Apostolate of the Laity*, no. 2).

Follower:

Yes, Holy Spirit, we have been told that evangelization is indeed the grace and the vocation that is proper to the Church. Evangelization constitutes her most profound identity. The Church exists for *evangelization*. She must preach and teach, as Pope Paul VI repeated it.

The Church must be the channel through which the gift of grace is transmitted. She

must reconcile sinners with God; she must per-
petuate the Sacrifice of Christ in the Holy
Sacrifice of the Mass which is a living memorial of Christ's Death and glorious Resurrection.

Holy Spirit:

Evangelization, like charity, must begin at
home, in the home of the human heart. The
Church is immersed in the world and is often
tempted by the idols and false gods that have
existed in every century. She must listen to the
records of the great works of God, the works
that have led to people's conversion.

People need constant renewals, and those
who make up the Church likewise constantly
need spiritual renewals.

Follower:

I cannot help admiring the Church founded by Christ and baptized by You, Holy Spirit.
She puts in the mouths of her evangelizers
wonderful saving words. She explains the
Divine message to them, a message of which
she is the depository. She gives to them the
mandate that she herself has received, and she
sends them to preach.

They are not sent by her to preach their
own gospel, their own ideas; they must preach
the Gospel.

Chapter 16
THE CHRISTIAN COOPERATIVE

Follower:

THERE are still people who imagine that the Pope and Bishops and priests *are* the Church. If this were true, it would not be difficult to accept that the Church is missionary, that she has the task of continuing Christ's work of evangelization, the task of preaching the Good News.

But that is not true. As we have seen, the faithful who constitute the majority in the Church are members of a missionary Church. They have a missionary task.

Holy Spirit.

It is well to go back to essentials. Human beings are clearly *social* beings. They normally need to be brought up, even for several years, in a family. By instinct, they form all kinds of civil and, quite naturally also, religious societies. In the Old Testament we have the "Chosen People," a religious Society. In the New Testament there is the Chosen People, also well called the (Mystical) Body of Christ.

In that religious Society all members are called to cooperate, to work together, to help one another for the common religious good of the members. In this sense they are already a cooperative, and a missionary cooperative.

Follower:

Perhaps, then, we can call our Church: A Christian Cooperative. St. Paul brings out the fact that just as in our body all the members, in various ways, must contribute to the "common good" of our human life, so must the members of Christ's Body, the Church, co-operate for the common spiritual good.

This, it seems to me, already shows that even in the members whom we call the faithful, the Church is *missionary*. All of us, Christians, participate in the task of building up, strengthening, improving the Church Society, the Church family, the Christian Cooperative. We can and must do this through good example and often also through words, through teaching.

Holy Spirit:

Of course, you must add that the Church through *all* her members must also seek to expand, to incorporate more and more human beings. The command: "Go, *therefore, and make disciples of all nations"* (Mt 28:19), though addressed first to a few "Apostles," is a project in which all the members of the Christian Cooperative must have more than simply an approving interest.

Think of the millions of human beings, created after God's image, who have not yet been informed about the Good News, or have not been taught to appreciate it, to desire it, and thus helped by grace to choose to become members of the Sanctifying and Saving Church!

There have been religious societies that accepted only few candidates. They were "exclusive" societies. Just the opposite is the case with the Church Society: it tends to be all-embracing, all-inclusive. It is a cooperative society that asks all members to cooperate in getting new members, and when possible to help in their instruction.

Follower:

We recall the words: "Woe to one who is alone," as well as the horrible expression: "Am I my brother's keeper?" The answer is, according to the will of the Father, the will of Christ, and Your Will, Divine Spirit: *Yes.* We must do what we can especially for the *spiritual* welfare of our fellow human beings.

There used to be an expression: "Alone with God alone." Contemplation, private, loving prayer to God, of course, is very good. But there is also the great commandment of loving our neighbor practically. And this does not mean merely loving our next door neighbor.

How well Jesus Christ taught us to be social-minded, cooperative-minded when He gave us, as a model prayer, the *Our Father*, a social prayer, a universal family prayer. We too easily forget or neglect to remind ourselves of the fact that all persons are potential members of the Church, and that we are asked to do what we can to achieve that universality.

Teaching the Good News by word and example begins at home, in the family. The family, we know, is the fundamental cell of civil society and also of our religious Society, the Church. Parents are the first Church-teachers, the first "missionaries," home-missionaries.

However, they must themselves be broad-minded in the sense that they are actively interested in the well-being of their neighbor, even in the welfare of those who live far away from them. In this respect you can learn much from the Church after Pentecost.

A Cooperative Prayer

H OLY SPIRIT, Substantial Love of Father and Son, pour Your Charity into us who were spiritually reborn, begotten of the Spirit, in Baptism.

Imbue us with a missionary, an evangelistic spirit, with the desire of sanctifying and sacrificing ourselves for the fulfillment of what Christ gave as His Last Will and Testament: *Teach all nations.*

Make us mission-minded. Make us pray for priestly and religious vocations. Make us pray that families may be small churches of prayer and of Christian charity, precious cells in the Body of Christ, the Catholic Cooperative founded by Christ, and animated by You, Holy Spirit.

For that purpose, help us to live holy Christian lives in imitation of Jesus Christ, and as true Followers of the Holy Spirit. Amen.

An Infant Teacher

I SHOULD never forget that the Church, sanctified by You, at the First Pentecost, is called the "Infant Church." Infant, we know, means speechless, as all new-born babies are. So it could be that when readers see the title above, they might consider it nonsensical.

Holy Spirit:

You know that the Church on and after Pentecost was a truly unique kind of "infant." That infant Church taught not only through the ministry of Peter and then through the other Apostles, but also through the faithful.

Follower:

On the First Pentecost, there was certainly a good deal of talk even in "tongues." We know also that the Infant Church grew with extraordinary rapidity, namely, in the number of her members.

Also, in addition to receiving Your inspiration and the teaching of the Apostles, the Christians, the recent converts, also attracted the admiring attention of Gentiles as well as Jews. *The entire community of believers was united in heart and soul* (Acts 4:32). Many sold their goods, becoming "communists" in the original sense of the term, as many religious today still choose to be, having all things in common.

Holy Spirit:

Note that they also prayed in common as was done by the Infant Church during the Novena before Pentecost. You have a saying that "a family that prays together also stays together"; this was true of the post-Pentecostal Church, for the members were prayerfully working together.

Recall what St. Luke tells you: *They [the converts] devoted themselves to the teaching of the Apostles and to the communal fellowship, to the Breaking of Bread [that is, taking part in the Eucharistic Liturgy] and to the prayers. . . . They would sell their property and possessions and distribute the proceeds to all according to what each one needed. Every day, united in spirit, they would assemble together in the temple. They would break bread in their homes and share their food with joyful and generous hearts. And day by day the Lord added to their number those who were being saved* (Acts 2:42-47).

Follower: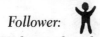

We know that there is much power in the apostolate of preaching through good example, for instance, by living a truly Christian family life. St. Luke is so enthusiastic about this that he repeats a description of the way the faithful lived: *The entire community of believers was united in heart and soul. None of them claimed any possession as their own, for everything was held in common. With great power, the Apostles bore witness to the Resurrection of the Lord Jesus, and they were all greatly respected* (Acts 4:32-35).

What a blessing to belong to a truly Christian, truly Catholic, Cooperative Society, founded by Jesus Who said: *"And when I am lifted up from earth [on the Cross], I will draw everyone to Myself"* (Jn 12:32). He had come to unite all human beings in one Great Family, not only for time but for all eternity.

CHAPTER 17

A COLLECTION OF PRAYERS

Follower:

DEAR Holy Spirit, the Infant Church was clearly prayerful. She was docile in learning from You through the instrumentality of Peter and the other Apostles. The faithful soon taught others by the example of their Christ-like lives.

The Church has outgrown her "infancy," but she continues to teach what we must believe and what we must do as followers of Christ and of You. One of the ways in which she does this is by her prayer-life, in accord with the old saying that the Praying Church is at the same time a Teaching Church.

Accordingly, I would like to give a number of prayers that are, at least in major part, copies of prayers that the Church uses for the celebration of the Sacrifice of the Mass and in the Liturgy of the Hours.

Holy Spirit:

That is an excellent idea. It is very important for people frequently to meditate on one or other of these prayers so that they may be penetrated by what they contain. It is quality not quantity of prayers that God wants. They must ask, with the Church: "O God, instruct us by the Light of the Holy Spirit, through meditative reading."

Eucharistic Prayers

1—O God, in this wonderful Sacrament You have left us a (living) Memorial of Your Passion. Grant us that, venerating the Sacred Mysteries of Your Body and Your Blood, we may constantly experience the fruit of Your Redemption. Amen.

2—O Lord, grant that we may everlastingly be filled with the enjoyment of Your Divinity. for this is prefigured in time by the reception of Your precious Body and Blood. Amen.

3—Heavenly Father, all life and all holiness come from You, through Your Son Jesus Christ, by the working of the Holy Spirit. May we be able to make a perfect (sacrificial) offering to Your glory. Amen.

4—Heavenly Father, grant that we who are nourished by the Body and the Blood (of Jesus Christ) may be filled with the Holy Spirit and become one body, one spirit in Christ. Amen.

5—Lord, may this Sacrifice, which has made our peace with You, advance the peace and salvation of the whole world. Strengthen the faith and the love of Your pilgrim Church on earth. Hear the prayers of the Family You have gathered. All glory and honor is Yours, almighty Father, through, with, and in Jesus, in the unity of the Holy Spirit. Amen.

6—Father, You so loved the world that You sent Your only Son to be our Savior. He was conceived through the power of the Holy Spirit and born of the Virgin Mary. That we might live no longer for ourselves but for Him, He (Jesus) sent the Holy Spirit from You, Father, to complete His work on earth and bring us the fullness of grace. Father, may this Holy Spirit sanctify us. Amen.

7—Almighty God, we pray that Your Angel may take this Sacrifice (of the Mass) to Your Altar in heaven. Then, as we receive from this Altar the sacred Body and Blood of Your Son, let us be filled with every grace and blessing. Amen.

8—Father, it is our duty always to give You thanks through your Beloved Son, Jesus Christ Who by the power of the Holy Spirit was born of the Virgin Mary. So with the Angels and the Saints we proclaim Your glory. May we who share in the Body and Blood of Christ be brought together in the unity of the Holy Spirit. Amen.

Prayers of the Liturgy of the Hours

9—O Lord, we beg You, may You always inspire us and continue to assist us so that whatever work we perform may always begin with You and may also be accomplished through Your assistance. Amen.

10—O God, You have told us that we must listen to Your Beloved Son. Nourish our inner self by Your Word so that, with a purified vision, we may (some day) rejoice in Your glory. Amen.

11—Lord, You are a God of mercy and the source of goodness. Teach us to make proper use of fasting, prayer, and almsgiving so that, because of our humble confession of our sinfulness, we may always enjoy Your merciful pardon. Amen.

12—Almighty and Eternal God, You have given mankind the perfect example of patience in Your Son become our Savior. He chose to become a Man and to die on a Cross. Grant that we may be inspired by His patience and eventually be granted to share in His Resurrection. Amen.

13—O God, it is supremely right that we should love You. Pour abundant grace into us, for through the death of Your Son, You have given us a foundation for our faith and our hope. May we, in virtue of His Resurrection, attain eternal life with You. Amen.

14—Lord, look kindly upon Your family, for our Lord, Jesus Christ, did not hesitate to deliver Himself to His executioners to undergo the death of the Cross. This we ask through Christ our Lord Who lives and reigns with You in unity with the Holy Spirit. Amen.

15—O God, by Your only Son, You have given us access to eternal life with You. Grant that we too may rise some day and enjoy eternal Light and Life through the Holy Spirit. Amen.

16—God of everlasting mercy, renew the faith of Your People and enlighten the minds of the faithful, that they may appreciate what You have revealed. For they have been redeemed by the Blood of Christ and have been reborn by the Holy Spirit. Amen.

17—God, by Your grace evil people are made righteous and wretched people are made happy. Be close to the works of Your hands. Fill people with Your gifts so that, animated by the gift of faith, they may also obtain the strength of perseverance unto the end. Amen.

18—Come, Holy Spirit, fill the hearts of Your faithful and enkindle in them the fire of Your Love. For by means of the diversity of tongues and in virtue of Your heavenly gifts You have deigned to gather the nations into the unity of faith. Amen.

19—O God, it is Your desire to sanctify all nations. Spread the gifts of the Holy Spirit throughout the whole world so that what was begun by the preaching of the Gospel may be abundantly diffused in the hearts of believers. Amen.

20—O God, You willed that Your Son should become Man in the womb of the Blessed Virgin Mary. Grant that we who believe her to be the Mother of God may be helped by her powerful intercession. Amen.

21—O God, You have given mankind eternal salvation through the fruitful virginity of Blessed Mary. May we experience the power of her loving intercession, for it is through her that we have received Jesus Christ Your Son, Who is the Author of Life. Amen.

22—O God, our hearts are open to You and You know our desires, for nothing is hidden from Your sight. Purify our minds by the infusion of the Holy Spirit so that we may love

You perfectly and desire to praise You worthily. Amen.

Private Prayers

1—O Holy Virgin, Mother of God, my Advocate and Patroness, I place myself under your protection and cast myself confidently into your merciful arms. Good Mother, be my refuge in my necessities, my consolation in my pains, and my advocate with your Divine Son, now, all the days of my life, and especially at the hour of my death. Amen.

2—Saint Joseph, Holy Apostles, and all our Holy Patron Saints, intercede for me that I may serve God faithfully in this life as you have done, and glorify Him eternally with you in heaven. Amen.

3—O my Guardian Angel, whom God in His mercy has appointed to watch over me, intercede for me that I may never stray from the path of virtue. Amen.

4—O Holy Spirit, Eternal Source of Light, dispel the darkness that conceals from me the malice of my sins. Grant me a lively sense of their enormity. Make me detest them with all my heart and dread nothing so much as to commit them hereafter. Holy Spirit, grant me the grace of making an act of Perfect Contrition. Amen.

Chapter 18

CHILDLIKE ABANDONMENT

Follower:

HOLY Spirit, I would like to talk with You about something I consider important for us Christians—and indeed for all people—namely, to act always as truly, supernaturally adopted children of God: *"Unless you change and become like little children, you will never enter the Kingdom of Heaven"* (Mt 18:3). Although this must seem silly to worldly people, especially the proud, it is an essential attitude for the true Christian.

There is an Association of the Holy Childhood, which prompts children to be generous in helping other children who are poor in material as well as spiritual goods, who do not know they have a loving Father in heaven, a Brother Who is the eternal Son of God become a Child for them, and a Holy Spirit Who is called "Father of the poor."

However, it is not about that very excellent Association of the Holy Childhood that I would like to talk, but about the "spiritual childhood" practiced and preached by St. Theresa of Lisieux who is known as the "Little

JESUS CALLS FOR CHILDLIKE QUALITIES—"Then
Jesus beckoned a child to come to Him, placed it in
their midst, and said: 'Amen, I say to you, unless you
change and become like little children, you will never
enter the Kingdom of Heaven'" (Mt 18:2-3).

Flower." She learned to act more and more as a child of God in the way Father, Son, and Holy Spirit want us all to act.

This means not only loving and obeying God but also having perfect confidence in Him. St. Theresa was the complete opposite of the completely self-reliant person whose number would seem to be constantly growing.

Theresa expressed in a sweet, poetical, feminine way the need of *abandoning* oneself entirely and unreservedly to God.

Holy Spirit:

Here again you cannot help noting how deficient human language is and how often virtually misleading. "Abandonment" and "abandon" can easily suggest giving something or someone up absolutely, as when one runs away giving up his arms or a fallen comrade who cried out for help. Why not explain what kind of abandonment you here have in mind?

Follower:

This is easy, for Venerable Francis Libermann, Superior General of the Holy Ghost Fathers, practiced and constantly preached this kind of abandonment during the first part of the nineteenth century, anticipating what was practiced and taught by St. Theresa in the second part.

Of course, neither of them invented this type of "abandonment." It is as old as Christianity. And in the Old Testament there were holy men and women who had the spirit of total confident abandonment to God.

There was also Father P. de Caussade who wrote an excellent book called: *Abandonment to Divine Providence.* I think the attitude of childlike abandonment to God is once more of the greatest importance because of the proud self-reliance of an increasing number of people. They seem to imagine that God is no longer necessary, for human science will eventually solve all of humanity's problems.

Holy Spirit: 🕊

You are right in stressing the need of spiritual childlikeness, of spiritual abandonment to Father, Son, and Holy Spirit. This is one reason for the insistence of Jesus on *praying always* (Lk 18:1) and thus constantly expressing one's dependence on God, one's confidence in God.

You chose the title: *"Following the Holy Spirit"* for your book. You could also have called it *"Abandoning Yourself to the Holy*

Spirit." Of course, that would have been a rather long title and harder to work with, but it would have reflected the contents of the book just as well.

Regarding the idea of "Following Me," you already recognized that it was suggested to you by what St. Paul, companion of St. Luke, wrote: *All those who are led by the Spirit of God are children of God. . . . The Spirit Himself bears witness with our spirit that we are children of God* (Rom 8:14-16).

Being led, of course, does not mean here being led involuntarily, like a lamb destined to be slaughtered. It means what you have expressed by the term "abandonment," like a child who with perfect confidence abandons itself to a loving mother.

Follower:

Holy Spirit, this is precisely what I want to emphasize, suggesting to readers that they should let You lead them. And they should do so not only by not offering any resistance to You but by committing themselves to You with a trust, a confidence that is absolute.

Holy Spirit:

There are persons who make the mistake of thinking they are letting themselves be guided by Me when they follow merely their own personal interpretation of the Bible. It cannot be sufficiently stressed that God works through human instruments and guides through human guides.

He guides children through parents and authentic teachers, and He guides Christians through the Pope, Successor of St. Peter and Vicar of Christ, and the Bishops in union with Him. *"Whoever listens to you listens to Me, and whoever rejects you rejects Me"* (Lk 10:16).

You already spoke about St. Theresa of Lisieux. Why not quote some of her words with respect to abandonment? It is unfortunate that attention to her form of "spiritual childhood" is not spread far and wide once more.

Follower:

Before giving the reader a sample of the way St. Theresa expressed her spirit of abandonment, which was the counterpart of her absolute confidence in God, it may not be out of place to remind ourselves that confidence in God is still written on all our coins and all our paper money: IN GOD WE TRUST! What a wonderful thing it would be if all those who use this money were constantly growing in such trust and on that account abandoned themselves wholeheartedly and unreservedly to God!

How many realize that when they carry our money they carry the *Name of God*; they are in a certain way *God-bearers*. Do militant atheists realize what they are carrying?

Here is the sample from St. Theresa:

O GOD, You chose a "mother" to create,
And are Yourself the very best of fathers.
Your Son incarnate is my perfect Love,
His Heart more kind than that of any mother.
He leads me and inspires me all day long;
And when I call in any kind of need
He kindly comes and helps without delay.
My Heaven? It is with You to be,
Safe in Your arms and resting on Your Heart—
Abandoning myself in perfect confidence
And fearing nought but from Your love to
　　stray.
My heaven?
It is with my Dear Lord to be!

Chapter 19

OTHER EXAMPLES OF ABANDONMENT

Holy Spirit:

YOU said that Venerable Francis Libermann was a model of spiritual abandonment to God during the first part of the nineteenth century. Why not tell your readers how
he expressed that spirit in words that were in
no way poetical, like those of St. Theresa?

Follower:

To understand the letter from which I shall
borrow a part it is necessary to mention that
Francis Libermann like St. Paul had suddenly
become a convert. Directly after his Baptism
he had expressed the desire to become a priest,
but epilepsy had prevented his ordination for
a good number of years, and he had mean-
while acted as novicemaster for the Eudist
Fathers.

Francis had been urged to found a Congregation to come to the spiritual aid of the most
neglected souls. He had just left the Rennes
seminary and was now preparing to go to
Rome. This letter is written to his brother, Dr.
Samson, and the latter's wife:

"I have left Rennes. I no longer have any creature on earth in whom I can place my trust. I have nothing and know not what will become of me nor how I shall even be able to live and survive. I shall, therefore, live a life that, according to worldly standards, is . . . lost.

"Very many disapprove of my conduct. I shall perhaps be treated as insane or as proud. Who on earth shall give me even a little bit of consolation? So I am a lost individual, unhappy for the rest of my life.

"That is the way worldlings reason. . . . If I had their mentality I should then be justified in making eternal lamentations. But, my dear friends, let us acknowledge that we *have a Father* in heaven! We have the most adorable Lord Jesus and His most admirable Mother.

"They will not *abandon* those who completely *abandon* themselves to them for their glory and their love. Therefore, have neither fear nor distrust. Acknowledge that *I am the happiest man in the world*, because I no longer possess anything but God, Jesus, and Mary.

"I already am in *heaven*, although still living upon earth. If it pleases God to make me lead a hard life, so much the better. He will give me *His* strength and *His* love, and that is all I need. My *only* hope is in Jesus and Mary. It should also be for you."

Holy Spirit:

No wonder you admire Father Libermann It is certain that he practiced what he preached or taught or counseled. He knew how to adjust his guidance to people in the world, to seminarians, to priests, or to missionaries. Like St. Paul, he never sought to impress his readers or his hearers by his eloquence, by his vast knowledge.

Why not give an example to show the way he taught *abandonment* to a seminarian?

Follower:

Here is a passage from a letter to a seminarian: "Cast yourself with total abandonment into the arms of Jesus, our Divine Lord. Feel certain that He will receive you. Keep in mind that you are weak. Battle as if you were certain that you will eventually overcome your difficulties.

"If you fall through weakness, quietly return to God; renew your courage by renewing your absolute confidence in our Lord and in the Most Holy Virgin Mary.

JESUS COUNSELS SELF-DENIAL—"Jesus then said to His disciples: 'Anyone who wishes to follow Me must deny self, take up the cross, and follow Me. . . . Those who lose their life for My sake will find it' " (Mt 16:24-25).

"Is it not wonderful that the Lord Jesus has so much patience and so much gentleness toward you? How foolish we are [in not putting all our trust in Him]? A blind man entrusts himself to the guidance of a small dog. But we, foolish creatures, more blind than those born blind, do not abandon ourselves to the guidance of a most clearsighted, most tenderhearted Divine Leader.

"To my mind this is the greatest possible blindness on our part. And how unjust we are to our most gentle and most lovable Lord Jesus!"

Holy Spirit:

There is no poetry in such texts but there is very precious and practical wisdom. No wonder Francis Libermann left thousands of letters of spiritual direction. His policy was first to consider things before God. Then after sufficient prayer and sufficient knowledge of a person he would show the person how I was guiding him or her.

He would point to the obstacles in the way of My spiritual activity in the person and inspire the desire and the will in the person to *follow the Holy Spirit.*

Follower:

It has been said that what was fundamental in Father Libermann's direction was *self-denial, abnegation.* But Bishop Gay, who had a unique knowledge of Libermann's life and writings, said that it was abandonment: the abandonment of a child of God, so well seen in the *little* Theresa who always remained a true *child of God.*

Holy Spirit:

In reality when there is total abandonment to another, total commitment to another, this demands total self-denial. Think of the matter of a choice: to choose to go and see a game is to *deny oneself* the pleasure of a good rest at home.

Recall what Jesus said: *"Anyone who wishes to follow Me must deny self, take up the cross, and follow Me"* (Mt 16:24). Abnegation and self-denial are unpleasant words, but look at what you get when you abandon yourself to God. You give up a small, temporal value for a value that is infinite and eternal: *God.*

Would it not be well now if you gave your readers the pleasure of reading a parable written by another Francis, namely, St. Francis de Sales, a most kind, most loving, and most self-giving bishop?

A Parable of Abandonment

Follower:

THIS I found in the Saint's *Treatise on the Love of God*. Physicians today are not fond of trying to cure a person by bleeding him or her, but it was the custom in former times. Here now is Francis' parable:

"The daughter of an excellent physician and surgeon was running a constant high fever. Knowing how greatly her father loved her, she told one of her friends: 'I suffer much, but I refuse to think of remedies, for I don't know what would be useful for my cure. Is it not much better for me to leave everything in the care of my father?

" 'He knows medicine. He knows what can be done and he certainly wants to do for me what is best. So why think about that, for he thinks about it for me. So I will wait until he decides such things.

" 'I shall only look at him when he stands near me and will express my filial love to him, showing my perfect confidence in him.'

"After saying this, the girl fell asleep. When she awoke her father was with her and asked her whether she desired him to administer a bleeding. . . . 'Father,' she answered 'I belong to you. It is you who should make the choice and desire for me all that you see to be right. As for myself, it is sufficient that I love you and honor you with all my heart, as I am doing.'

"So the father pierced the vein and made the blood flow, but the girl did not look at her bleeding arm. She looked only at her father's face and merely murmured from time to time: 'My father loves me greatly. I belong entirely to him.' When the operation was over, she did not express thanks to him but merely repeated once more the same words full of affection and filial confidence.

"Now, tell me, my dear friend Theotime [i.e., one who has filial fear of God], did that girl not manifest a more solid love for her father than if she had taken great care to question his remedies for her illness and if she had looked with concern at her bleeding arm instead of looking at him?

"If she had expressed many words of gratitude, she would have practiced only the virtue of gratitude. Did she not do much more and please her father infinitely more by

manifesting her [absolutely confident] love
to her father?"

What charm and simplicity there is in this
Parable, and how well it illustrates the fundamental point! Abandon yourself wholly and
with perfect confidence to your Heavenly
Father, to Jesus, to the Holy Spirit, as was done
by St. Theresa of Lisieux, Venerable Libermann, St. Paul, and, yes, millions of others
who now are forever beloved children united
with the Divine Family that exists eternally.

Holy Spirit:

You easily see how that wonderful confidence is connected with Faith and with Hope.
You know *in Whom [you] have placed [your]
trust, and [you are] confident* (2 Tim 1:12) — to
use the words of St. Paul. You recite properly
the Act of Hope saying: "Relying on Your infinite goodness and promises, I hope to obtain
the pardon for my sins, the help of Your grace,
and life everlasting."

With Faith in God disappearing today
among people, Hope likewise disappears, for
its solid foundation is taken away.

Follower:

Dante writes that he saw written over the
gate of hell: "All you who enter, leave all hope

behind." It is virtually written over the gate of the Communist Eden. The godless used to express their contempt for the foolish hope of Christians with the words: "Pie in the sky when we die." It is ironic that many of their political prisoners have not even pie upon earth before they die.

In contrast, those who continue to believe and hope in God know for certain that the Risen Christ will give them a Divinely made Eden: *Eye has not seen, ear has not heard . . . what God has prepared for those who love Him* (1 Cor 2:9)—those who, serving Him perseveringly, put all their trust in Him, and practice the great and fundamental virtue of *holy abandonment.*

Chapter 20
PRAYERS OF CONFIDENCE

1. Prayer of St. Theresa

LORD, I recognize how weak I am, but every day I recognize in my weakness an occasion for salutary (confidence). You deign to impart to me the wisdom that makes me "glory in my infirmities."

This is a very great grace. In it I find peace and rest for my heart. I have now learned to know Your "character": You give as being God, but You expect from us *humility*.

2. Prayer of St. Augustine

LORD Jesus Christ, Son of the living God! On the Cross, with arms extended, for the redemption of humanity, You drank the bitter cup of intolerable sufferings. Help me, who come as poor to You Who are rich, as wretched to You Who are merciful. Prevent my ever leaving You. Feed me and grant me the grace of being truly nourished by You. Amen.

3. Prayer of St. Mary Magdalene de Pazzi

YOUR Providence, O Lord, is so great that You take care of all Your creatures as if there were only one, and You take care of each one as if all others were enclosed in it.

If people could only understand and recognize Your [all-embracing] *Providence* and that they can unite themselves to [an all-providing] God! How different their ideas of earthly values would be! Grant us absolute confidence in You, most Merciful God! Amen.

4. Prayer of St. Mary Magdalene de Pazzi

O LORD, it is your Spirit Who helps me in my interior battle. You have given me Your Spirit to enable me to kill the works of the flesh in me. Moved by your Spirit, I continue the struggle, and the reason is that I have Your powerful assistance.

Lord Jesus, You have accepted to be wounded for me and by Your Death You have overcome my death. You are the strength that makes me unshakable in the presence of temptations. You are my refuge, my hope, my heritage in the land of the living. Amen.

5. Prayer of St. Mary Magdalene de Pazzi

O LORD, give me a strong *hope*, for I cannot attain salvation without that virtue being deeply rooted in my soul. This hope is necessary that I may ask for You to pardon my sins and that I may reach my [supernatural] end.

How greatly this hope gladdens me, making me firmly expect that I will attain heaven, my homeland. Even in this life it gives me a fore-taste of relishing, understanding, and possessing You, my God. Amen.

6. Prayer of St. Francis of Assisi

LORD, make me an instrument of Your peace.
Where there is hatred, let me sow love.
Where there is injury, let me sow pardon.
Where there is friction, let me sow union.
Where there is error, let me sow truth.
Where there is doubt, let me sow faith.
Where there is despair, let me sow hope.
Where there is darkness, let me sow light.
Where there is sadness, let me sow joy.
O Divine Master,
grant that I may not so much seek
to be consoled as to console,
to be understood as to understand,
to be loved as to love.
For it is in giving that we receive.
It is in pardoning that we are pardoned.
It is in dying that we are born to eternal life.
Amen.

Prayer Inspired by the Holy Spirit

Follower:

I HAVE quoted a number of prayers composed by holy men and women, mostly canonized Saints. What I should like to do, for the benefit of the readers, is to recall prayerful writings that were directly influenced by Your supernatural inspiration, O Holy Spirit.

Some years ago there was a pastor and writer, who considered it preferable to leave out the subject of Hope! No doubt there is not one Saint who would agree with such a declaration. On the contrary, I am sure, all agree that Hope is one of the most precious infused virtues and that what people need more and more in our own day is precisely the development of that virtue.

Let me then quote some important texts inspired by You that powerfully bring out its supreme value. There is first the sad condition of hopelessness:

1. "Blessed Is the Man Who Places His Trust in the Lord"

CURSED is the man who places his trust
in human beings,
and relies on *human* strength,
while his heart turns away from the Lord.

Such a person is like a shrub in the desert;
  when relief comes, he will not be aware of it.
He will continue to live
  in the parched areas of the desert,
  in an uninhabited salt land.

        In contrast with such a man:

Blessed is the man who places his *trust* in the
    Lord,
  and whose *hope is the Lord.*
He will be like a tree planted by the water
  that spreads out its roots to the stream:
When the heat comes, it does not fear;
  its leaves stay green.
It is not concerned in a year of drought,
  and it never fails to bear fruit (Jer 17:5-10).

2. "In Hope We Were Saved"

FOR in Hope we were saved.
  Now to see something does not involve
    Hope.
For why should we Hope for what we have
    already seen?
But if we Hope for what we do not yet see,
then we wait for it with *patience.*

In the same way, even the Spirit helps us in
    our weakness,
For we do not know how to pray as we should,

but the Spirit Himself intercedes for us . . .
because the Spirit intercedes for the saints
in accordance with God's will (Rom 8:24-27).

3. The Hope Placed before Us

WHEN God desired to show even more
clearly to the heirs of His promise
the unalterable nature of His purpose,
He confirmed it by an oath.
Therefore, by these two unchangeable acts
in which it was impossible for God to lie,
we who have taken refuge in His protection
have been strongly *encouraged*
to *grasp firmly the Hope* that has been held
    out to us.

We have this Hope as the anchor of the soul,
a Hope that enters the sanctuary behind the
    veil,
where Jesus has entered as a Forerunner
on our behalf,
having become a *High Priest forever*
according to the order of Melchizedek (Heb
    6:17-19).

Chapter 21
LOVE

Follower:

HOLY SPIRIT of light and love, You are the substantial Love of Father and Son; hear my prayer:

Bounteous Bestower of most precious gifts; grant me a strong and living *Faith*, which makes me accept all revealed truths and shape my conduct in accord with them.

Give me a most confident *Hope* in all Divine promises, which prompts me to abandon myself unreservedly to You and Your guidance.

Infuse into me a *Love* and a *Charity* of perfect goodwill, which makes me accomplish God's will in all things and act according to God's least desires. Make me love not only my friends but my enemies in imitation of Jesus Christ Who through You offered Himself on the Cross for all human beings.

Holy Spirit, animate, inspire, and guide me, and help me to be always a true follower of the Holy Spirit. Amen.

Holy Spirit:

You know that Father, Son, and Holy Spirit always listen and give answer to people's prayers in accord with what is in line with God's designs and is for the eternal good of the petitioners.

Follower:

I have had the pleasure to talk with You about Hope. I like the way our acts of Faith, Hope, and Charity are worded. In the Act of Hope I like the mention of its foundation: "Relying on Your *infinite goodness.*" Can we find a stronger and more perfect foundation than that?

It is about this goodness and love that I should like to talk with You.

I have presented a good number of prayers, and there is one thing that all their authors had in common: they greatly loved God and greatly loved their "neighbor." Augustine was a lover already when he was a young man, but it was for some time more in the nature of a selfish love. We might even question whether he had a genuinely selfless love for his mother at that time.

On the other hand, St. Monica always loved her son with a love of goodwill, a self-sacrificing love. And when Augustine ran away from her and sailed for Italy, she pursued him, as the "Hound of Heaven" pursues souls.

And Augustine, pursued by an ever-praying mother, finally gave in and became a most wonderful lover of God and neighbor.

"Love, and do what you please" is the way Augustine expressed this new outlook on life. And in writing such a maxim he was no longer speaking of the selfish kind of love. He was speaking of true love of God and neighbor.

Holy Spirit:

You are right. There are people who "love" solely for their own satisfaction. They regard loving others as "taking" rather than "giving."

You sometimes speak of Christ as the Divine Bridegroom, Who *loved* His Bride, the Church, and *gave Himself up for her, in order to sanctify her* (Eph 5:25-26). You also know the word: "*No one can have greater love than to lay down one's life for one's friends*" (Jn 15:13). And He laid down His life not only for His friends who were few in His time on earth but also for His enemies.

As a result, Paul, a persecutor of Christ in His members, learned to know and love Christ and Him crucified. How great a lover Paul became! After breathing vengeance, he breathed

NO GREATER LOVE—Jesus said to His disciples: "This is My commandment: love one another as I have loved you. No one can have greater love than to lay down one's life for one's friends" (Jn 15:12-13).

self-giving love. The kind of love he preached to others he himself practiced.

Why not recall some of the things he wrote, which came from the abundance of his loving heart.

Follower:

St. Paul has written so many things that express his love that I have great difficulty in choosing among them. One of his sayings I like very much is: *The love of God has been poured into our hearts through the Holy Spirit Who has been given to us* (Rom 5:5). Here is *a giving love, a giving goodness.*

And how greatly Paul liked to quote the words of Jesus that are found only in Acts, i.e., Luke's "Gospel of the Holy Spirit": "*It is more blessed to give than to receive*" (Acts 20:35). Christ was the happiest of people because having become Man He went about doing good. Indeed, He did unbelievable good "unto the end," which was no end at all, for Christ continues to give Himself though in an unseen way.

Allow me now, Holy Spirit, to recite *the Act of Love,* which I like very much:

"O my God, I love You above all things, with my *whole* heart and soul, because You are infinitely perfect and worthy of all my love. I love my neighbor as myself for the love of You. Amen.

Holy Spirit:

Why not explain the fundamental motives for loving God that are expressed in this prayer. You have already mentioned that there is a kind of "loving" of another that in reality is a form of self-love. You will do well also to bring out what relation there is between perfect love and perfection—which is something everyone, with the always available Divine help, should strive to attain.

Follower:

Dear Holy Spirit, I should like to have recourse here to St. Francis de Sales, a genuine lover of God, who gave us his great *Treatise on the Love of God.* One thing I noticed is that, like the Venerable Francis Libermann, he does not end with love in his spiritual direction but begins with it. St. Francis, of course, says similar things about love or charity, in his *Introduction to the Devout Life*, which has been read, loved, and put into practice by millions.

He first tells us that many seek perfection in the wrong way. They also call perfection things that are only a *means* to perfection, such as austerities and saying many prayers.

Austerities, mental prayer, and other exercises of virtue are very good *means* to make progress in perfection, but what is all important is that they must be practiced *in charity, in love* and out of a *motive of love.* Charity is the only virtue that unites us to God and to neighbor in the way God desires.

What then is our means to reach perfection? The answer is very simple. Our Lord. told us to love God with our *whole heart* and to love our neighbor as ourself. And what is the way, what is the means I must use to arrive at perfection?

Here again the answer is: Charity, Love. This is a wonderful virtue for it is at the same time a *means* and an end, a *goal.* What is the shortest way, the easiest way, the best means of loving God with our whole heart? It may, sound foolish but it is simply this: by truly loving God with all our heart.

We learn studying by studying, cooking by cooking. We learn speaking by speaking—and so we learn to love God and our neighbor by *loving them* (that is, by daily practicing love, unselfish charity).

And what is "loving God and neighbor"? It is willing what is good, *for* God Himself and *for* our neighbor. It is the love of absolutely unselfish *goodwill*.

We thus love God, first for what He has and is, rejoicing that He is and possesses those things: His Goodness, His Power, etc. And then we wish Him the honor and obedience that are due Him on the part of His creatures.

The words "All for the greater glory of God" should not be a dead letter on the top of a sheet of paper. We should truly, self-sacrificingly do and suffer all things for His greater glory. We will then, at the same time, do all we can to make others honor, serve, and love Him.

To love our neighbor is to rejoice in what our neighbor has that is good and useful for God's glory. It means assisting that neighbor whenever possible. It means being zealous for the spiritual, for the eternal well-being of the neighbor, and doing all this because God wants it, because God loves everyone.

So we repeat: Perfection consists in having and practicing true charity, loving God firmly and sincerely out of love for Him, and secondly loving our neighbor for love of God.

Chapter 22

LOVE FOR NEIGHBOR

Holy Spirit:

WHY not let your readers know how love for one's neighbor is most intimately connected with love for God? You will find this well expressed by St. Francis de Sales.

Follower:

Dear Holy Spirit, perhaps you are referring to these thoughts found in his *Treatise on the Love of God.*

God has created human beings in His *image* and *likeness.* Hence, He has commanded that we should love them in the *"image and likeness"* of the love we owe to God: " *'You shall love the Lord your God with all your heart. . . .' This is the greatest and first commandment. The second is like it: 'You shall love your neighbor as yourself.' "* This we are told by Jesus Christ (Mt 22:37-38).

Why do we love God? According to St. Bernard, the "cause" or reason why we love God is God Himself, so as to say: we love God because He is sovereign and infinite goodness.

Why do we love ourselves through Charity? It is certainly because we are the *image and likeness of God.* Now, because all human beings have that same dignity, we love them also *as we love ourselves,* that is, because they are all most holy and living images of the Divinity. For it is in virtue of this quality (of *images* of God) that we belong to God in a most intimate alliance with Him and in such a loving dependence on Him that He has no difficulty in calling Himself our Father and in calling us His children.

It is in virtue of this (being *images* of God) that we can be so united to His Divine Essence, enjoying (eventually) His sovereign goodness and blessedness.

It is in virtue of this (being *images* of God) that we receive His *grace* and that, in a certain way, we are made sharers in His Divine Nature, as we are told by Pope St. Leo the Great.

It is, therefore, in this way that the same Charity that produces the acts of love for God produces similarly acts of love for our neighbor.

To love one's neighbor through Charity is to love God in people, or to love people in God. It is: to love God alone for love of God Himself, and to love creatures out of love for God.

Holy Spirit:

Some readers might find these words somewhat ponderous and difficult. Why not now give the readers what was proclaimed and testified by St. Jeanne de Chantal, who knew St. Francis de Sales so very well?

Follower:

Someone has said: "Words call us but examples draw us." The writings of St. Francis call us, but his example, his conduct, draws and attracts us most powerfully. St. Jeanne de Chantal who knew him so very well made the following "Deposition," witnessing to his extraordinary charity:

"Francis de Sales spent and shortened his life in serving his neighbor. He frequently interrupted his meal and shortened his sleep for that service. He undertook labors and bore inconveniences that others would have considered absolutely unbearable.

"He never refused anything to anyone. No matter at what hour anyone came to see him and however important the thing he was occupied with, he never sent away those who desired to speak to him, nor did he manifest any disgust or annoyance because of what visitors came to talk about. He said: 'To poor people small things appear as important as great affairs appear to "great" people.'

"He received in this way all kinds of persons, always with a gracious countenance and such affable words that his visitors readily unburdened themselves with perfect confidence. Never did anyone leave him without feeling perfectly satisfied; and all who came always bore with them admiration for his incomparable charity. . . .

"When visitors happened to be uncouth or boorish, he acted as if he did not notice such things.

"I have seen him suffer foolishness and bad tempers that were absolutely unreasonable. It seemed that that blessed man lived only for the service and the consolation of the neighbor."

Holy Spirit:

I suppose that when you witness such perfection of self-sacrificing love for one's neighbor, you say to yourself: Why can I not act like that? And the answer is: You can. Did not St. Paul say: *I can do all things in Him Who strengthens me* (Phil 4:13)?

The perfect example, of course, of self-sacrificing charity toward any neighbor is Jesus Who said: *Learn from Me, for I am meek and humble of heart* (Mt 11:29).

Paul became "another Christ," so did St. Francis of Assisi, and so did innumerable men and women who virtually knew nothing but *"Jesus Christ—and Him crucified"* (1 Cor 2:2). Think of St. John of the Cross, of St. Teresa of Avila.

Read the lives of the Saints—but not lives that are written "as literature" and by authors who in no way try to imitate the example of the one whose life and conduct they describe. Read, as much as possible, lives of Saints written by holy writers who like St. Francis de Sales make you admire and imitate the virtues of holy men and women.

Chapter 23

MARY, EXEMPLAR OF LOVE FOR GOD

Holy Spirit:

ONE way of learning how to love God and neighbor the way you have described it is by meditating on the words and actions of Jesus Christ. Another way of achieving this end is by meditating on the love and charity of Christ's Mother, the most loving and most beloved of all women. She has so often expressed that love when appearing to persons on earth at places where there now is a shrine and a church dedicated to Christ and His Mother.

People like to read about these apparitions and many sick people visit the shrines in the hope of being cured. Some return home not cured of their physical illness as they had prayed and hoped, but loving God more because they were now accepting their crosses.

People also prefer reading stories to reading theological treatises, which sometimes are drier than dust. Why not recall a good story now in reference to the Mother of God?

MARY OUR INTERCESSOR WITH JESUS—The wine ran out and Jesus' Mother told Him, "They have no wine." Jesus told the waiter to fill six jars with water and take some to the chief waiter, who tasted it and found it to be choice wine (Jn 2:3-11).

Follower:

I recall one told me by Monsignor Hawks, an Episcopalian priest who became a convert and pastor of a church in Philadelphia. Coming back one day to the rectory, he was met by the lady at the desk who told him that the small paper she showed Father had been found on the floor just inside the door. It read: "Please come to . . . ." Monsignor Hawks went to the place and knocked at a door of a particular house. He asked the woman who opened the door: "Did you send for me?" She answered: "No . . . ," and then added: "It might be the woman upstairs."

Monsignor went upstairs, knocked at the door, and on entering asked a woman who was lying in bed and evidently very ill: "Did you send for me?" The sick woman answered: "No, Father. I am not a Catholic." Monsignor then moved back toward the door, but the woman said to him: "Father, do not leave. The Lord must have sent you."

Sitting near the bed, he listened to her story. She always liked Catholics. Everything Catholic was good! After some time Monsignor noticed she had a rosary wrapped around her wrist. To his questioning she answered: "I found this one day outside a Catholic Church. It was broken. I have worn it ever since."

After a long conversation with the woman, Monsignor found out that she knew the fundamentals of the faith and he had the joy of hearing the sick woman say she would like to become a Catholic and die as a Catholic.

He told her he would come back the following morning and administer the Sacraments to her. The lady replied, showing evident anxiety: "No! No! Father, my husband, you see, is badly disposed. . . ." Monsignor replied: "I will come tomorrow morning!"

On his return the next morning, a rather ferocious looking man opened the door—the husband—but Monsignor virtually hypnotized him ordering him to carry a burning candle before him as he ascended the stairs. As Monsignor entered the room, he saw "visitors" sitting in a circle around the room. They were preparing to assist at the death of their friend.

Monsignor first explained to them what he intended to do for the sick lady. He then administered the Sacraments and after giving her the Viaticum started to blow out the candle, but the sick lady begged him: "Please, Father, don't blow out the candle; the *Lord is still in me!*"

One year later, Monsignor went into a bakery on the opposite side from the house where he had ministered to the sick lady. The woman in the bakery told him: "Well, that woman got the priest last year, didn't she? Monsignor replied: "But she was not a Catholic!" "She *was a Catholic*," the woman replied. "When she came in here and I gave her a loaf of bread, I saw she carried the beads on her arm. She *was a Catholic!*"

Of course, the lady of the bakery was the one who had sent the message to Monsignor Hawks. There are Catholics who have given up the wonderful practice of reciting the Blessed Rosary! They do not realize how much they are missing.

How grateful we should be to our Lady who deigned to teach children at places like Lourdes and Fatima how to pray the Rosary devoutly, meditatively. She showed how to honor the Father, the Son, and the Holy Spirit and how to intercede for sinful people, asking help from her who is both God's Mother and ours!

Holy Spirit:

A right kind of devotion to our Lady leads not only to love for God but also to love for neighbor.

Chapter 24

DEVOTION TO MARY

Holy Spirit:

ALL human beings are made after the image of God, but many do not "develop" that image by imitating the God-Man, by imitating Mary, St. John of the Cross, St. Thomas More, St. Catherine of Siena, and other Saints. Why not tell your readers what St. Francis de Sales wrote about some who stood near the Crucified Savior?

Follower:

Here is one text that might be appropriate:

"Several holy persons were present at the death of the Savior. Among them, those who had the greatest love for Him also had the greatest sorrow. So, His Mother who loved Him most suffered more than the others: her heart was truly pierced with a sword of grief.

"The pain suffered by the Son was like a sword passing through the heart of the Mother, for her heart was in the closest union with the heart of her Son and nothing was able to wound the one without wounding the other.

"Now, Mary not only did not seek a remedy for her wound, but she loved her wound more than any cure, for she constantly desired to die from that wound, because it was from it that her Son had died, willing to be a whole burnt offering for the sins of people. . . .

"Let us then remain that way in the darkness of the Passion of Christ. Our Lady stood near the Cross in horrible darkness.

"She no longer heard our Lord. She no longer saw Him and she was filled with sorrow and distress. Though she remained full of faith, she was at the same time in darkness, for she was called to share in the Savior's dereliction.

"She knew, however, that this was the Will of the Heavenly Father. This was enough to make her remain firm at the foot of the Cross, accepting that her Beloved should die."

(Treatise on the Love of God)

Hail, Holy Queen

HAIL, Holy Queen, Mother of Mercy, our life, our sweetness, and our hope. To you we cry, poor banished children of Eve. To you we send up our sighs, mourning, and weeping in this vale of tears.

Turn, then, most gracious Advocate, your eyes of mercy toward us. And, after this our exile, show to us the blessed fruit of your womb, Jesus. O clement, O loving, O sweet Virgin Mary.

Pray for us, O Holy Mother of God, that we may be made worthy of the promises of Christ. Amen.

The Hail Mary

SAINTS cannot stop proclaiming the beauty and the power of the Hail Mary. There is no other prayer that honors Mary more.

When we repeat with the Angel Gabriel, the messenger sent by the Holy Trinity, the words: "Hail, Mary" (Lk 1:28—a newer translation is: "Rejoice), we are repeating the greeting that the All-Holy God brought her. We thus make her recall the joy that flooded her when she heard the heavenly message. It was with these words that our work of salvation began.

When we say the words: "full of grace" (Lk 1:28—a newer translation is: "O highly favored daughter"), we remind Mary of her Immaculate Conception and all the virtues with which Divine Goodness adorned her, as with a diadem and glorious mantle.

And, as was revealed to Blessed Eulalia, she always experiences extraordinary joy at the words: "The Lord is with you" (Lk 1:28), for it is as if Jesus were still in her (as in His temple).

When, after that, we repeat with the Angel: "Blessed are you among women" (Lk 1:28), we remind Mary with what respect and love her name is spoken, the name of the Queen of the world. For, after God and Jesus, Mary has the greatest power; she has the greatest wisdom and the greatest mercy.

The words of Elizabeth: "Blessed is the fruit of your womb" (Lk 1:42), make her recall the intention and purpose of Almighty God when He chose her to be, as it were, co-redemptrix, the living channel of grace for the unfortunate children of Eve.

The third part of the Hail Mary, which is the Church's prayer, begins with the words "Holy Mary," which can have various meanings: Star of the Sea, or Ocean of Sorrow.

And immediately we add to it what are Mary's great privileges. Through her Divine Motherhood ("Mother of God"), the Fathers of the Church tell us, Mary was taken up into the Family of the Holy Trinity and was established as a Mediatrix between God and humans

The consideration of this extraordinary greatness makes our hearts humble, and we spiritually bow before her and say, "Pray for us sinners."

When Mary sees that we so humbly invoke her, it is to be expected that she will have compassion for us and that she will listen to our prayer when we say: "Now and at the hour of our death."

Unbelievably great is the influence of the Hail Mary and its power to make Mary be gracious to us and to grant us all that we ask her to obtain for us.

When we fervently pray, she looks with tenderness upon us, for in the Hail Mary we mention all the graces with which the Holy Trinity enriched Mary. That is why it is well for us to practice the frequent repetition of the Hail Mary.

Chapter 25
THE GIFT OF GOD

Follower:

COME, Holy Spirit, fill the hearts of the faithful and kindle in them the *fire* of Your *love!*

Dear Holy Spirit, I should like to meditate on what the beloved Disciple, St. John, says about You. Jesus puzzled Nicodemus, a member of the Sanhedrin, when He told him that *"no one can enter the Kingdom of God without being born of water and the Spirit"* (Jn 3:5). Nicodemus did not understand that the Divine Master was referring to a wonderful *gift of God.*

Later, Jesus revealed Himself as a good shepherd rescuing lost sheep, as bringing to sinners a supreme *gift of God.* I am now referring to that most inspiring story of the Samaritan woman, a true story that has made millions of people truly enthusiastic, which means "animated by God."

Holy Spirit:

There are no useless details in this account of the meeting and the conversation of Jesus, the Holy One of God, with the sinner. It shows how thoroughly human Jesus had desired to become—His real fatigue, His real need of a rest, after a long journey; and now it was midday, and He felt the need of a drink of water.

Nothing was casual in this meeting. From all eternity, just as Mary of Nazareth had been chosen to be His immaculate Virgin Mother, that Samaritan woman had been predestined to become an exemplary, contrite, and believing convert.

You also see the primacy of the spiritual over the natural, the sacrifice of one's own comfort for the sake of healing and nourishing another with something that is Divine.

You cannot help noticing how Jesus gradually passes from the natural to the supernatural. He does not, at the very start, accuse the woman of being a sinner. He puzzles her, virtually prompting her to talk with a Jew. He excites her curiosity. He shows extreme patience throughout and, with a loving smile and gentleness, makes her realize that He already knows everything about her sinful condition. He asks her to give Him a drink of water. . . .

Why not now tell your readers what you like to bring out for their benefit in the story of the Samaritan woman?

Follower:

How gracious You are, *Spirit of love!* I should like to recall what St. Augustine, that wonderful convert, brought out in his *Treatise on St. John's Gospel,* regarding Christ's dialogue with the Samaritan woman. Here is part of what he says: "He [Jesus] Who asked for a drink of water thirsted for the woman's faith."

After He had asked for a drink' Jesus said to her: *"If you recognized the gift of God and Who it is that is asking you for some water to drink, you would have asked Him and He would have given you living water"* (Jn 4:10).

"Christ," Augustine continues, "asked to have a drink and He promised a drink. He was in need of something and He was ready to satiate another."

And what is the *gift of God* that our Lord desired the sinful woman to know? Augustine answers: "The *Gift of God is the Holy Spirit.* Jesus, therefore, promised the woman a very special kind of food: an *overabundance of the Holy Spirit. . . ."*

We know that the woman, quite naturally, at first failed to understand the magnificence of Christ's promise. But why is it that we Cath-

GOD'S GIFT OF THE SPIRIT—"Jesus replied [to the Samaritan woman], 'If you recognized the gift of God and Who it is that is asking you for some water to drink, . . . He would have given you living water [that is, an overabundance of the Holy Spirit]' " (Jn 4:10).

olics—at least those who have been sufficiently instructed—are not truly "enthusiastic" about that *gift of God*?

Dear Holy Spirit, instruct, enlighten us,
Christians, and make us ever more appreciate Your Heavenly, Your Divine gift.

Holy Spirit, make us all practically believe
in the fact of Your indwelling in the souls of
the just. Let us often ponder the words of St.
Paul: *The Spirit of God dwells in you. Anyone
who does not possess the Spirit of Christ cannot belong to Him. . . . If the Spirit of Him
Who raised Jesus from the dead dwells in you,
then the One Who raised Christ from the dead
will also give life to your mortal bodies
through His Spirit Who dwells in you. . . . All
who are led by the Spirit of God are children
of God* (Rom 8:9-14).

Holy Spirit:

You said that you would tell the readers
what St. John the Evangelist says about My
mission to human beings. Pope Paul VI said
well, on one occasion: "The Church *needs*
the Holy Spirit: the Holy Spirit in us, in each
of us, and in all of us together, in us *who are
the Church.* . . . Let all of you ever say: [Holy
Spirit,] come!"

JESUS PROMISES TO SEND THE HOLY SPIRIT —
"I will ask the Father, and He will give you another
Advocate to be with you forever, the Spirit of Truth
Whom the world cannot accept. . . . [He] will teach you
everything" (Jn 14:16-17, 26).

Follower:

St. John, who wrote under Your inspiration, Holy Spirit, tells us that Jesus said: *"I will ask the Father, and He will give you another Advocate [that is, Paraclete, Coach, Prompter] to be with you forever, the Spirit of Truth Whom the world cannot [refuses to] accept. . . . [He] will teach you everything"* (Jn 14:16-17, 26). *"He will guide you into all the truth"* (Jn 16:13).

It would be strange if the Beloved Disciple who became the guardian of Christ's Mother, of her who was the "Spouse of the Holy Spirit," would not refer to You in his Letters.

We all know how full of love—inspired by You—John reveals himself to be, in his First Letter. He begins by expressing his exuberant love for Christ repeating the same things over and over again, as lovers frequently do!

That which existed from the beginning, which we have heard, which we have seen with our own eyes, which we have looked at and touched with our hands: we are speaking of the Word of life. . . . What we have seen and heard we declare to you so that you may have fellowship with us (1 Jn 1:1-3).

We . . . [are to] love one another just as [God] commanded us. All those who keep His commandments abide in Him, and He abides in them. And the proof that He abides in us is the Spirit that He has given us (1 Jn 3:23).

Similarly, John tells us: *This is how you can recognize the Spirit of God: every spirit [person] that acknowledges that Jesus Christ has come in the flesh is from God* (1 Jn 4:2).

Then John, as was his custom, repeats over and over again that we must love one another: *God IS LOVE. . . . Since God loved us so much, we too should love one another. . . . If we love one another, God lives in us, and His love is brought to perfection in us. This is how we can be certain that we abide in God and that He dwells in us: He has given us a share in His Spirit* (1 Jn 4:8-13).

For good measure, let me add these words of St. Jude: *In the final age there will be scoffers who will follow their own ungodly lusts. These worldly people are the ones who create divisions and do not possess the Spirit. . . . Build yourselves up on the foundation of your most holy faith and pray in the Holy Spirit* (Jude 18-20).

Chapter 26

INSPIRED AND INSPIRING THOUGHTS

Follower:

DEAR Holy Spirit, we know that You inspired the writers of the Bible, the greatest
book in the world. We are told that *all Scripture is inspired by God and is useful for teaching, for refutation, for correction, and for
training in uprightness, so that the man of
God may be proficient and equipped for good
work of every kind* (2 Tim 3:16).

We are told also that *God did not give us a
spirit of timidity but rather a spirit of power
and of love and of wisdom* (2 Tim 1:7).

When these sacred writers give us spiritual
counsels, may we not say that You are coun-
seling us, for it is God's custom to use instruments for the transmission of His commandments, His counsels, His sacred teaching?

1. Man of God, . . . pursue righteousness,
godliness, faith, love, fortitude, and gentleness. Fight the good fight of faith (1 Tim 6:
11-12).

2. Rejoice always. Pray continually. Give thanks in all circumstances. For this is the will of God for you in Christ Jesus (1 Thes 5, 16-18).

3. My brothers, we beg you to respect those whose duty it is to labor among you as your leaders in the Lord and to admonish you. Hold them in the highest possible esteem and affection because of their work (1 Thes 5:12-13).

4. Pray too that we may be rescued from wicked and evil people, for not all have faith. However, the Lord is faithful. He will strengthen you and protect you from the evil one (2 Thes 3:2-3).

5. Fight the good fight with faith and a good conscience. Some people have spurned their conscience and destroyed their faith (1 Tim 1:18-19).

6. I urge then, first of all, that supplications, prayers, intercessions, and thanksgiving be offered for everyone, . . . for all those who hold positions of authority, so that we may be able to lead a tranquil and quiet life with all possible devotion and dignity (1 Tim 2:1-2).

7. God . . . desires everyone to be saved and come to full knowledge of the truth. For there is one God, and there is one Mediator between God and human beings, Christ Jesus, . . . Who gave Himself as a ransom for all (1 Tim 2:3-6).

8. Wonderful, indeed, is the mystery of our faith, as we say in professing it: "He [the Son of God] was made visible in the flesh, vindicated by the Spirit, seen by Angels; proclaimed to the Gentiles, believed in throughout the world, taken up in glory" (1 Tim 3:16).

9. Train yourself in godliness. While physical training has some value, the benefits of godliness are unlimited, since it holds out promise not only for this life but also for the life to come (1 Tim 4:7-8).

10. The love of money is the root of all evils, and in their eager pursuit of wealth some have wandered away from the faith and pierced themselves with many serious wounds (1 Tim 6:10).

11. For we brought nothing into this world, and we can take nothing out. . . . Those who are searching for riches fall into temptations and are trapped (1 Tim 6:7-9).

12. Avoid the profane chatter and the contradictions of what is wrongly considered to be knowledge. By professing it some people have strayed far from the faith (1 Tim 6:20-21).

13. God did not give us a spirit of timidity but rather a spirit of power and of love and of wisdom. Therefore, you should never be ashamed of bearing witness to our Lord . . .

Rather, you should utilize the strength that comes from God to share in my hardships for the sake of the Gospel (2 Tim 1:7-8).

14. God saved us and called us to a life of holiness, not because of anything we had done but according to His own purpose and the grace that has been bestowed upon us in Christ Jesus from all eternity (2 Tim 1:9).

15. This saying can be trusted: If we have died with Him, we shall also live with Him. If we endure, we shall also reign with Him (2 Tim 2:11-12).

16. Avoid idle and worldly chatter, for those who indulge in it will become more and more ungodly, and their teaching will spread like a plague (2 Tim 2:16-17).

17. There will be great distress in the last days. People will love nothing but themselves and money. They will be . . . arrogant, . . . disobedient to their parents, ungrateful, irreligious, . . . lovers of pleasure rather than lovers of God. . . . Avoid persons like that (2 Tim 3:1-5).

18. The time is coming when people will not accept sound doctrine, but they will follow their own desires and listen only to those teachers who will preach what their itching ears want to hear. They will shut their ears to the truth and be captivated by myths (2 Tim 4:3-4).

19. The time has come for my [Paul's] departure. I have fought the good fight; I have finished the race; I have kept the faith. Now waiting for me is the crown of righteousness (2 Tim 4:6-8).

20. [Jesus] saved us through the bath of rebirth and renewal by the Holy Spirit, Whom He lavished on us abundantly through Jesus Christ our Savior, so that we might be justified by His grace and become heirs in hope, of eternal life. This saying can be trusted (Tit 3:5-8).

21. Let your minds be filled with whatever is true, whatever is honorable, whatever is just, whatever is pure, whatever is pleasing, whatever is commendable, whatever is excellent, whatever is worthy of praise (Phil 4:8).

22. Let us never grow weary of doing what is right, for if we do not give up, we will reap our harvest in due time. Therefore, while we have the opportunity, let us labor for the good to all, but especially to those members of the household of the faith (Gal 6:9-10).

23. None of us live for ourself, and none of us die for ourself. If we live, we live for the Lord, and if we die, we die for the Lord. Therefore, whether we live or die, we are the Lord's (Rom 14:7-8).

Chapter 27
FIDELITY

Follower: ✝

DEAR Holy Spirit, reading Jeremiah 7: 27-28 I could not help saying to myself that something similar is taking place in our own day with respect to unfaithfulness. Here is what I read: *This is the nation that did not obey the Lord, its God, or accept correction. Truth has perished. It no longer issues forth from their mouths.*

We still use the word and there remain many people who are faithful to God and faithful in relation to their neighbor. But in many nations there is an increasing practice of unfaithfulness.

Think of the number of divorces, and of infidelity to the marriage vows. Think of the many priests and religious who, although they knew what they were doing when they made vows or promises, have broken them, a scandal to young and old, a grief to Mother Church, an insult to the infinitely good God Who made them after His own image and likeness and died for them.

We know that one of the Apostles became more than unfaithful to the most kind Master. But we must repeat: There go I, were it not for God's grace. We are weak, fallen creatures, inclined to evil from our youth.

One thing all should ask of God: How can we prevent unfaithfulness, infidelity toward God, in relation to our neighbor, for instance in marriage? What should we do so that we shall not break our promises, not discard what we have knowingly, earnestly made?

Holy Spirit:

You know the answer. God gave the answer in the Old Dispensation and, in later times, Christ the Son of God Who became also totally human taught faithfulness by all His conduct and His preaching. Some today almost forget or even deny Christ's Divinity.

Christ, eternal Son of God, did not have to fear becoming unfaithful to His Heavenly Father, unfaithful to His promises, to the task He had accepted to undertake. Jesus could not sin as the Tempter foolishly thought He could and would. Why not now continue along this line of thought?

Follower:

Having chosen to become a "servant," Jesus humbled Himself in Nazareth, faithfully obey-

ing Mary and Joseph, His creatures. He be
came obedient unto death, faithfully obedient unto death, dying in association with
condemned criminals.

Christ, surely, did not have to pray in order
to remain faithful. He humbled Himself insist-
ing on being baptized in a baptism of *repentance*, administered by John the Baptist, in the
presence of penitents. But, *as He was praying,*
You, Holy Spirit—appearing as a dove—gave
witness to Him, and to Your silent testimony
the Father added: *"This is My beloved Son, in
Whom I am well pleased"* (Mt 3:17).

Before starting His public life, Christ did
not have to spend forty days in a prayerful
retreat, nor did He have to pray in order to be
able to overcome the devil's clever "Scripture-
based" temptation.

What then was Christ's purpose in manifesting His humble prayerfulness? The
answer is very simple: *"I have given you an
example"* (Jn 13:15), and *"Learn from Me"*
(Mt 11:29).

Holy Spirit:

You brought out well the importance of
prayer. *Ask, and it will be given to you* (Mt 7:7).

THE POWER OF TRUSTFUL PRAYER — "Jesus answered them, 'Amen, I say to you, if you have faith and do not permit any semblance of doubt, ... [and] you say to this mountain, "Be lifted up and thrown into the sea," it will be accomplished. Whatever you ask for in prayer and do so in faith, you will receive' " (Mt 21:21-22).

228

When you ask for faithfulness toward God, and faithfulness with respect to your neighbor, there is no reason for God to refuse such a grace. Prayer, therefore, persevering, humble prayer is one great means for remaining *faithful.*

You rightly pointed out that although the Son of God became perfectly human, He could not possibly sin. But He came as an exemplar for a truly Christian life, and so He made use of prayer, which is a fundamental need, an absolute necessity, for people who can exercise free choices.

As you also already pointed out, human beings are weak and need special help in order to persevere in doing what is right. God wants them to ask for help, and by appealing to God for help they at the same time practice something fundamental. They declare their dependence on God, Creator, and therefore Absolute Lord, in reality Owner of every creature.

Follower:

Holy Spirit, we are repeatedly told those things not only for God's glory but also at the same time for our eternal blessed life with God. In spite of that, some so-called Chris-

tians virtually declare their independence of
God.

When the Holy Father reminds them of
fundamental commands and prohibitions
regarding moral conduct, or recalls fundamental beliefs, they sit in judgment on the Vicar of
Christ and reject those fundamentals, thereby
becoming unfaithful, while claiming they still
belong to the Catholic "faithful."

The way some behave regarding the Holy
Sacrifice of the Mass, the reception of Holy
Communion, and the Sacrament of Reconciliation, which requires humble confession of
sins, constitutes an expression of *unfaithfulness.*

Some today worship more attentively and
obediently at the altar of Television than at the
wonderful Christian altar. A good number
seem to have become sinless, going habitually
to Holy Communion and refraining from first
becoming reconciled to God through seeking
pardon for grievous sins.

We are told by the Divinely inspired writer
that the fear of the Lord is the beginning of wisdom (Ps 111:10). Do those who reject fundamentals of our Holy Religion, those who make
wicked use of Mass and Sacraments still have
any wholesome fear of the Lord?

Does it ever come to their minds that sudden death—so frequent nowadays—could bring them before the tribunal of a Just God? Can they expect that He would greet them with the words: *"Well done, good and faithful servant. . . . Come and share your master's joy"* (Mt 25: 21)?

To play with fire is dangerous. To play with things that are abominable in the eyes of God is infinitely more dangerous. So I ask myself what can be done.

Holy Spirit:

You know the answer with respect to your own behavior and what you would like to suggest to others. Keep up the practice of *daily* devout, humble, confident prayer.

You know how much prayer your particular work permits. You can work prayerfully, doing everything for God. Perhaps you can say at least part of the Rosary every day. Read lives of Saints. Of course, read meditatively short texts in Holy Scripture, particularly in the New Testament.

You follow a rule regarding your work in the home or outside of it. Have a rule also with respect to your prayers, the reception of the Sacraments, and spiritual reading.

Religious have a Rule and formerly they were told: Keep the Rule and the Rule will keep (safeguard) you. This is true also for people in the world. You should act according to the motto of St. Joan of Arc: *God served first!*

Formerly suggestions were made by preachers of retreats and "missions": pray three Hail Mary's when you get up in the morning. Say three Hail Mary's before going to bed at night. Daily examine your conscience and prayerfully say the act of Contrition, an act of *perfect contrition*.

Follower:

Here again examples are more powerful than words to make us act rightly, to make us remain faithful. Examples are innumerable. God—Father, Son and Holy Spirit—is faithfulness!

God wanted freewill creatures. He promised them guidance, formation, sanctification, and salvation. God never fails to fulfill His promises and He reminds human beings of this on many occasions.

God is an ever faithful Bridegroom in spite of the infidelity of His "bride." You, Divine Spirit, are ever ready to pardon truly repentant sinners in spite of repeated sins, repeated unfaithfulness of human beings.

St. Peter writes (1 Pet 4:19): *And so, those who suffer in accordance with God's will have entrusted their souls to a faithful Creator, while continuing to do good* (1 Pet 4:19). In the Book of Revelation (1:5), Christ is called by the beautiful name of *the faithful witness*.

Thanks be to God, not only canonized Saints have been wonderful in their faithfulness. There are countless others who lost their lives in martyrdom or accepted sometimes a very long martyrdom of sufferings and sorrows.

How beautiful and joyful the death of those who have remained faithful to the end! Does not Jesus the "faithful witness" receive each one of them saying: Come, enter, faithful witness?

Chapter 28
CALLS TO FIDELITY

Holy Spirit:

YOU have spoken about the much-needed practice of faithfulness in imitation of God: Father, Son, and Holy Spirit, in imitation also of so very many saintly men and women. Faithfulness to God and neighbor is a grace and this grace must itself constantly, faithfully be prayed for and pursued.

It must be assiduously sought as people daily seek food and drink. Hunger and thirst remind them of the necessity of regularity, of daily satisfying the needs of the body. In the spiritual order there are human-made reminders. Religious are called by the bell to various exercises. Many use alarm-clocks, which the French call "awake-morning."

Follower:

Holy Spirit, I think I know what You are suggesting. You want me to tell my readers about mottos, maxims, axioms, as reminders, as animators. Let me then ask myself what were some of the dominant ideas, judgments, and their expressions by which people were inspired and lived. We find these can also act as prompters for groups, societies, and nations.

I could start with the GOD-MAN (where there is the difficulty of choice), then our Lady, the Apostles, the early Christians, etc.

1 — *I always do what pleases Him* (Jn 8:29) — *I came that they might have life and have it to the full* (Jn 10:10).

2 — *I am the servant of the Lord* (Lk 1:38).

Of course, our Lord did not need reminders. Perhaps our Lady did not need any either, but it is good for us to be reminded of fundamental attitudes and aims of Christ Who is the Way, and of Mary, Christ's and Your so very faithful follower.

3 — They *"were of one heart and one mind"* (Acts 4:32) became later the motto of the Spiritan Congregation.

4 — (St. Peter:) *"To whom shall we go? You have the words of eternal life!"* (Jn 6:68).

5 — (The doubting Apostle:) *"My Lord and my God!"* (Jn 20:28).

6 — (St. Paul: — Difficulty of choice!) *"I [will] speak of nothing but Christ and Him crucified"* (1 Cor 2:2) — *"It is more blessed to give than to receive"* (Acts 20:35).

7 — (John the evangelist, the disciple whom Jesus loved:) *"God is love"* (1 Jn 4:8).

8—(James:) *"Faith without works is futile"* (Jas 2:20).

9—(St. Augustine:) "Love, and do what you please."

10—(Constantine:) "In this sign [the Cross] you will conquer!"

Holy Spirit:

There is a French saying: "Those who cannot limit themselves cannot teach [well]." So there is no need of recalling the mottos or reminders used by *many* wonderful Christians.

The important thing is to make use of some motto that powerfully reminds you of your chief duties, which can make you enthusiastic about walking in the steps of the Divine Master, and following My inspirations.

Follower:

In line with Your suggestion, dear Holy Spirit, I shall confine myself to mentioning just a few more.

11—(Words of a Jesuit Saint who died young:) "What is this in relation to eternity (how insignificant, therefore)?

12—(St. Thomas Aquinas) "Who is like God?"

JESUS ALWAYS DOES HIS FATHER'S WILL —
"When you have lifted up the Son of Man, then you
will realize that I AM, that I do nothing on My own
authority and I say nothing except what the Father has
taught Me. . . . He has not left Me alone for I always
do what pleases Him" (Jn 8:28-29).

13—(Teresa of Avila:) "To suffer or to die."

14—(Theresa of Lisieux:) "Abandon yourself wholly to God."

15—(Libermann:) "God is all. We [of ourselves] are *nothing*."

Holy Spirit:

You know that many, reading one particular sentence in the Bible, choose it for their motto. This brings out the fact once more that it is not useful to act upon a multitude of mottos.

When you have found one that truly inspires you to be faithful make use of it as long as it does animate and inspire you.

Follower:

That is why I like the motto, or is it a proverb: "Not MANY things, but MUCH"—in other words, "Do not get lost in quantity, but seek quality."

Dear Holy Spirit, Counselor, would You be so kind as to suggest some considerations which might be spiritually beneficial to the readers?

Chapter 29

JOSEPH, FAITHFUL SERVANT

Holy Spirit:

YOU have spoken with me about faithfulness. There is one who, entering heaven, heard the words that fitted him *perfectly*: You are a *"good and faithful servant. . . . Come and share your Master's joy"* (Mt 25:21).

He was a man of few words. In fact, not one word of his has been recorded. But his conduct speaks more loudly than any words. He was not a wealthy man. He was not an educated man. But he was a conscientious man, a workman who always did his work carefully and well.

It was a famous woman, a nun, who called attention to him making the Church authorities pay more and more respect to that man. He lived in a despised town, in obscurity. No record has been preserved for you regarding where and when he died.

By this time, you know very well about whom I have been speaking.

Follower:

Yes, Divine Teacher. It took the Church a long time to give him the very special honor he deserves. It was a woman, the Carmelite nun Teresa of Avila, who started a movement of special devotion to *St. Joseph,* that was to culminate later in his being designated "Patron of the Church."

His solemn Feast is now celebrated on March 19, two days after that of St. Patrick. What a contrast between the missionary Bishop and that "ordinary" family man.

St. Joseph must have been a most humble, and a most patient man. Matthew tells us how he was informed belatedly about Christ's unique conception:

[Mary] was found to be with child through the Holy Spirit. . . . An Angel of the Lord appeared to him in a dream and said, "Joseph, son of David, do not be afraid to receive Mary into your home as your wife. For this Child has been conceived in her womb through the Holy Spirit" (Mt 1:18-20).

Joseph showed no impatience. He did not complain to the Angel: "Why did you not tell me this before it happened? I would not then have had the trouble of mind that I under-

ST. JOSEPH: DILIGENT AND FAITHFUL SERVANT OF GOD—As long as he lived, St. Joseph protected Jesus and Mary and diligently supported them by his work as a carpenter. He obeyed every word God made known to him (see Mt 1:18-25, 2:13-15, 19-23).

went when I found that my betrothed was
with child!"

When there was no decent place for the
unique Child to be born in, he did not cease
to believe in the extraordinary Mystery.
When he was told to flee with the Child and
the Mother, he did not say to himself: Is the
Lord of Heaven not powerful enough to protect us in our house at Nazareth?

In spite of all that Mary had told him about
the Child, he continued to support that extraordinary family by the work of his hands. He
sought the Child, sorrowing, when the Child
had been lost. He saw with what respect, with
what obedience, this Boy was subject to His
creatures.

And that sort of thing went on for many,
many years. But Joseph kept the faith and
Joseph remained faithful—one of the greatest
and most perfect examples of faithfulness!

Holy Spirit:

Devotion to St. Joseph (like Devotion to
Mary) is particularly necessary today when you
see the degradation and degeneration of family life. Teresa of Avila said well that other Saints
are particularly invoked for one or other need.

St. Joseph can and should be invoked for anything you need in the physical and the spiritual
order.

"Go to Joseph" was the advice people received when the Joseph of Egypt was admin-
istrator and provider at a time of widespread
famine. Sold by his brothers, he later repaid
them with unbelievable kindness and generosity.

No wonder that many Congregations of religious have been dedicated to St. Joseph, and
very many churches also. How sad that an
increasing number of Christians no longer have
Saints' names before their family names. How
salutary to bear always the name of an inspiring
Saint! And such surely is that of St. Joseph!

Follower:

Perhaps it would be proper to give the readers the great Prayer, spread far and wide, by
Pope Leo XIII, who at the end of his life gave
us his magnificent Encyclical on the Holy
Spirit. That Vicar of Christ reigned from 1878
to 1903. He had been a great defender of the
working class. He was, of course, also a great
preacher of sound Devotion to Mary, Mother
of Jesus, wife of St. Joseph.

Prayer of Pope Leo XIII to St. Joseph

TO YOU Blessed Joseph, we have recourse in our affliction, and, having implored the help of your thrice-holy Spouse, we now, with heart filled with confidence, earnestly beg you also to take us under your protection.

By that charity wherewith you were united to the Immaculate Virgin Mother of God, and by that fatherly love with which you cherished the Child Jesus, we beseech you and we humbly pray that you will look down with gracious eyes upon that inheritance which Jesus Christ purchased by His Blood, and will help us in our need by your power and strength.

Defend, O most watchful Guardian of the Holy Family, the chosen offspring of Jesus Christ. Keep from us, O most loving father, all blight of error and corruption.

Aid us from on high, most valiant defender, in this conflict with the powers of darkness; and even as of old you did rescue the Child Jesus from the peril of His life, so now defend God's holy Church from the snares of the enemy and from all adversity.

Shield us ever under your patronage, that, following your example and strengthened by your help, we may live a holy life, die a happy death, and attain to everlasting bliss in heaven. Amen.

Prayer of St. Teresa to St. Joseph

DEAR Joseph, how much I love you! How I like to think of your life that was so simple and so humble! You have lived by faith, as we do. . . .

A long experience has taught me what graces you can obtain for us from God. That is why I would like to convince all people that they should have great confidence in you.

I have not known a single person who had a true devotion to you, and who honored you in a special way, who did not make progress in virtue. . . . I do not recall that at any time I have not immediately received what I had asked you to obtain for me. . . .

Since our Lord was obedient to you, St. Joseph, upon earth, He likewise answers granting what you ask for now. . . .

Dear St. Joseph, it is with complete confidence that I place myself under your protection. Teach me to live like you, by faith and by abandoning myself to God. Teach me to live solely for Him, by consecrating myself completely to His service. Amen.

Chapter 30

THE SPIRIT OF GOD USES
THE POOR AND LOWLY

Follower:

DEAR Holy Spirit, I can understand why St. Teresa of Avila and millions after her have found great inspiration in meditating upon the life and conduct of St. Joseph: his humility, his obedience, his patience, his reliance on Divine Providence, his fidelity to his family, the most extraordinary family in the history of mankind.

Petty critics might say: Why did God treat him that way? Why was the Church so slow in giving him special honors in her worship?

Just as Teresa of Avila said that he can be invoked for everything, so is he now also a model for married people and for celibates, for those in authority and for subjects. Though head of the Family, he acted always as a servant—a most faithful servant.

Another thing that comes to my mind is that Joseph (like Mary) brings out the fact that God seems to like to use for His instruments those whom the world despises. From all eternity God chose a workman who no doubt had little money and had to work hard to provide food and clothing for his family.

If he had had enough money, he could no doubt have found someone in Bethlehem to let him stay in the inn or in a private home, especially when Mary was expected to give birth to a child.

You, Holy Spirit, are called the "Father of the poor." This does not mean that all poor people are holy by that fact. They might be jealous and envious, unfaithful to God, mean to their neighbor. However, Almighty God seems to like to choose those who are not self-sufficient, those who have a hard time to make their living, as well as the uneducated.

He seems not to want those who pride themselves on their deep knowledge, their "science." And He accomplishes wonders through seemingly unfit, unsuitable instruments.

Why choose men who merely knew how to catch fish, as was the case with several of the Apostles? And this sort of thing is repeated throughout the centuries. It would be interesting to find out how many souls were converted, sanctified, and saved through the instrumentality of some of the great pulpit orators and then compare that figure with the number of converts made by St. John Vianney, the so-called ignorant Curé of Ars, for example.

St. Paul, who was an educated man, did not consider it useful to study under Greek philosophers in order to catch many souls for Christ. He realized that God chooses the seemingly useless ones to produce "much fruit."

This does not mean that human sciences cannot be used beneficially. It means, as Venerable Francis Libermann insisted on repeating, that souls will not be converted by merely clever, learned people, but by holy people, that is, people inspired by You, Holy Spirit, Who impart Divine wisdom and Divine love for God and neighbor.

Great was the number of converts made by "ignorant fishermen." Furthermore, neither Mary nor Joseph was a priest, and neither was highly educated. Yet who can estimate the enormous influence both of them have exercised for the spiritual well-being of those who were prompted to become followers of Christ and followers therefore also of You, Holy Spirit?

You are the spiritual Director par excellence, the Divine Counselor, and, like Father and Son, You make use of frail instruments to achieve Your purposes. Is it not true that some rely too much on human means, on human organization, on merely natural advertisements to obtain vocations, to transform people, to make human beings resemble Christ more and more?

Who has been God's counselor? Only in heaven shall we be given an understanding of the ways of God. But God's ways are already manifested in the choices God is pleased to make of men like St. Joseph, of women like St. Margaret Mary Alacoque.

Powerful electricity can pass through seemingly powerless wires. God's grace can be transmitted through seemingly powerless persons. Nevertheless, God wants holy transmitters of grace and sanctification.

The holiness of parents, of religious, and of priests attracts sinners and makes them eager to receive the Divine graces that God is pleased to transmit through weak human instruments.

Holy Spirit:

You are right in emphasizing the importance of the example of Joseph, the carpenter of Nazareth. *"Can anything good come from Nazareth?"* (Jn 1:46). *"Is this [Jesus] not the carpenter's Son?"* (Mt 13:55).

You are right: God's ways are not human ways. Men and women must accept God's ways as was done so perfectly by the husband and his spouse in the Holy Family of Nazareth.

St. Paul understood this well. Recall what he said to the Corinthians: *I did not proclaim to you the mystery of God with words of eloquence or "wisdom." . . . I came to you in weakness. . . . My message and my proclamation were designed to convince you not with persuasive words of "wisdom," but with the power of the Spirit, so that your faith might rest not on human wisdom but on the power of God. . . .*

God has revealed these things to us through the Spirit. . . . The Spirit we have received is not the spirit of the world but the Spirit Who is from God (1 Cor 2:1-5, 10-12).

Chapter 31

ANGELS AND THE ANGELUS

Follower:

ST. JOSEPH, Mary's husband, and the fos-ter-father of Jesus, had certainly a most wonderful privilege of living so close for many years to the Son of God become Man and to Mary become the "Mother of God." This must have made up greatly for what he suffered when he discovered that his betrothed was pregnant, when there was no room for them in the inn, and when he had to go into exile in Egypt.

Mary and the Child were certainly consolation enough for him, but to them was added also the consolation coming from what are called "Angels." These are "sent from God" and happen to be particularly privileged beings since they always see the face of God (see Mt 18:10), always enjoy what we call the *Beatific Vision.*

When Joseph was troubled, having discovered that Mary *was found to be with child, . . . an Angel of the Lord appeared to him in a dream and said, "Joseph, son of David, do not be afraid to receive Mary into your home as your*

ST. JOSEPH AND ANGELS—"An Angel of the Lord appeared to him in a dream and said, 'Joseph, son of David, do not be afraid to receive Mary into your home as your wife. For this Child has been conceived in her womb through the Holy Spirit' " (Mt 1:18-20).

wife. For this Child has been conceived in her womb through the Holy Spirit" (Mt 1:18-20). This makes me think that St. Joseph must have had a particular love for Angels and great devotion to You Who had done such very great things in and for Mary, Your Spouse.

Holy Spirit:

It is sad to see some Christians who virtually do not believe in Angels and others who acknowledge that they exist but pay absolutely no attention to them. As you say, St. Joseph loved Angels. He was most grateful to them and admired their loving ministry, their service of God, service of Christ, and service of people.

Follower:

I spoke about reminders. Bells are good reminders, and the Church has made great use of them — to remind people of services in the church, of the deaths of parishioners, etc. Then, of course, in many Catholic countries, there was the Angelus bell, which three times a day recalled the wonder of the Incarnation.

The "Angelus" is the Latin word that expresses the Scriptural account: *The Angel [Angelus] Gabriel was sent . . . to a virgin* (Lk 1:26-27). It seems that at first when the bell rang, three Hail Mary's were said, particularly by religious. To these prayers later on were added the fundamental words expressing the Incarnation: The Mystery of a Son of God become Son of Mary, Son of Man.

Holy Spirit: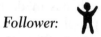

Pope Paul VI is well known for having fostered devotion to the Angelus, by calling people together and adding to prayers a short spiritual talk, which is afterward broadcast all over the Christian world through the *Osservatore Romano*, the Vatican newspaper.

The Angelus is such a very simple thing, but, when said respectfully, attentively, and devotedly, it can be a great inspiration to people in all sorts of conditions, regarding their needs of the body and their needs of the soul.

Follower:

I always liked a famous painting by the great French artist Millet who showed a husband and a wife standing in a field and with bowed heads reciting the Angelus. At a great distance one sees the steeple of a church whose spire points heavenward. In this painting, with a minimum of means, the artist conveyed a maximum of expression and inspiration. In all

probability, the couple had heard the church.
bell proclaiming the Angelus, the fundamental
mystery of Christianity: the *Incarnation*.

If we reflect on the words of the Angelus
(which are given below), we will see that
through it we honor not only Jesus and Mary,
not only an Angel, but also You, dear Holy
Spirit!

The Angelus

℣. The Angel of the Lord declared unto Mary.

℟. And she conceived *by the Holy Spirit*. Hail,
Mary, full of grace, the Lord is with you.
Blessed are you among women and bless-
ed is the fruit of your womb, Jesus. . . .
Amen.

℣. Behold the handmaid of the Lord.

℟. Be it done unto me according to your word.
Hail, Mary . . . .

℣. And the Word was made flesh.

℟. And dwelt among us.
Hail, Mary . . . .

℣. Pray for us, O holy Mother of God.

℟. That we may be made worthy of the promises of Christ.

Let us pray

Pour forth, we beseech You, O Lord, Your
grace into our hearts; that as we have known

the Incarnation of Christ Your Son by the message of an Angel, so, by His Passion and Cross, we may be brought to the glory of His Resurrection, through Christ our Lord. Amen.

Follower:

How simple and at the same time how rich in meaning and inspiration for young and old, for men and women, for persons in any profession, is the *Angelus!* And how sad to think that there are so-called Catholics today who reject the *Incarnation*, which means they deny that the Eternal Son of God became Man.

Holy Spirit:

St. Thomas Aquinas, the Angelic Doctor, had no difficulties with either the Incarnation or Angels. And when you study both Old and New Testament writings prayerfully and with an open mind, you will say to yourself: how is it possible to have any doubts about Angels, and how is it possible to neglect seeking the help, protection, and inspiration of spiritual beings who are so close to God, who too were made after the image of God, and who were and remain ever faithful to God?

Follower:

I recall with joy what Jesus tells us: *"Take care that you do not despise one of these little*

JESUS AND ANGELS—Jesus said to His disciples: "Take care that you do not despise one of these little ones, for I tell you that their Angels in heaven gaze continually on the face of My heavenly Father" (Mt

18:10).

ones, for I tell you that their Angels in heaven gaze continually on the face of My heavenly Father" (Mt 18:10).

Even Satan, that fallen Angel quoted Holy Scripture, and in this case that arch-liar virtually affirmed truthfully the existence of *faithful* Angels when he told our Lord: *"Scripture has it: He will bid His Angels take care of you"* (Mt 4:6).

How is it possible for a believing Christian to feel lonesome? We are never alone. You dwell in us, Christ remains the Emmanuel, the God with us, and we have Angels to transmit God's messages to us and to protect us.

When Charles Lindbergh had successfully crossed the Atlantic Ocean in his frail plane, one newspaper had a picture of the vast ocean and high up in the sky there was what looked like a bird, Lindbergh's plane, and the caption read: *Alone.* But he was *not* alone.

We are never alone, although those ready to help us are unseen as You, Holy Spirit, are unseen. They are always ready to counsel, console, and guide us, and there is no excuse for us if we are not faithfully *following the Holy Spirit.*

Do we not read in the Epistle to the Hebrews (1:14): *Are not all Angels ministering spirits, sent forth to serve for the sake of those who are destined to inherit salvation?* Does not the Holy Spirit-filled Luke tell us (15:10): *There is rejoicing among the Angels of God over one sinner who repents?*

And so we join the Angels and the Saints in proclaiming Your *glory* as we sing:

Holy, holy, holy Lord, God of power and
    might.
Heaven and earth are full of Your glory.
Hosanna in the highest.
Blessed is He Who comes in the Name of the
    Lord.
Hosanna in the highest. Amen.

Chapter 32

THE SPIRITUAL RENEWAL
OF THE CHURCH

Holy Spirit:

YOU know that something of greatest importance today is a genuine spiritual
renewal of the Church. People need to know
what the Church on earth truly is and what
God expects of all the members. You have
Holy Scripture and you have the recent decla-
rations of Vatican Council II that can show
how great is the importance of greater holiness
on the part of Christians.

Follower:

Pope John XXIII desired a new Pentecost,
which clearly meant a spiritual renewal of the
members of Christ's Mystical Body. He evidently did not mean a physical repetition of
what happened at Jerusalem on that first Pentecost:

*There came from heaven a sound similar to
that of a violent wind, and it filled the entire
house in which [the Apostles and others] were
sitting. Then there appeared to them tongues
as of fire, which separated and came to rest on*

each one of them. All of them were filled with the Holy Spirit and began to speak in tongues (Acts 2:1-4).

What Pope John wanted was that Christians should most generously follow Your guidance, O Holy Spirit, pray to You, invoke You, and accept to be led by those who in the Church are successors of St. Peter and of the other Apostles, whose invisible head is Christ, and whose soul You are, O Holy Spirit:

Those whom He foreknew He also predestined to be conformed to the image of His Son, so that He might be the Firstborn among many brothers and sisters (Rom 8:29).

As was well expressed in Vatican Council II: "He [the Father] planned to assemble in the holy Church all those who would believe in Christ. That Church has been announced in figures from the beginning of the world. It had been wonderfully prepared in the history of the People of Israel and in the Old Covenant. It was finally established in later times.

"It was manifested thanks to the effusion of the Holy Spirit and, at the end of the centuries, it will be completed in glory. To that union with Christ, Who is the Light of the world, from Whom we proceed, through Whom we live, toward Whom we tend, all are called."

Holy Spirit:

The Church Council revealed well in those words God's design regarding human beings and the origin of the Church as she exists upon earth. Why not also quote St. Paul who points to the infinite mercy of the Father Who chose people in Christ?

Follower:

In his Epistle to the Ephesians, St. Paul, full of enthusiasm, exclaims: *Blessed be God, Father of our Lord Jesus Christ, Who has blessed us in Christ with every spiritual blessing in the heavens. Before the foundation of the world He chose us in Christ to be holy and blameless before Him and to be filled with love. He also predestined us for adoption as His children through Jesus Christ. . . .*

He has made known to us the mystery of His will . . . that He predetermined in Christ to be realized when the fullness of time had been achieved: namely, the plan to bring all things, both in heaven and on earth, together in Christ as the Head (Eph 1:3-10).

Holy Spirit:

Notice that it is from all eternity, from before the creation of the world, that the Father decided to make His "rational creatures" His *adopted children,* in Him Who is His Only Son by nature and Who, in due time, was to assume a human nature. Christ the Lord! And this marvelous destiny, which is the effect of His infinitely merciful love, would remain even after mankind's Fall, for in Christ the sinner would find *redemption* and *remission of sins.*

Follower:

Holy Spirit, how weak are our human words to express such sublime truths. How difficult for us to understand the *gift of God!*

There we have the design of the infinitely loving Father regarding the world: to bring back all things under one Head, the Christ, which means to recapitulate all creation in Christ, in the Word become flesh, in order to form the *People of God* in a definitive way, namely, the everlasting *Church of heaven.*

We know that the Holy Spirit is the soul of the Church whether on earth, in purgatory, or in heaven. Reflecting now only on the Church upon earth, we know that the Church owes to the Holy Spirit her existence, her character, her organization, her growth and all her supernatural activity. So we are permitted to say that, according to the Church's Founder, the Church is unthinkable apart from the Holy Spirit.

Chapter 33

VATICAN COUNCIL II SPEAKS OF THE SPIRIT

Follower:

IT HAS occurred to me, dear Holy Spirit, that this book might profitably contain a chapter giving some of the magnificent texts that Vatican Council II set down about You, about Your work, Your inspiration, and Your grace. Naturally, it would be impossible to give all the texts. Therefore, I appeal to You to help me make a suitable choice.

Holy Spirit:

What you suggest seems to be a fine idea. You have already told your readers many things about Me. However, a selection of texts from the Council is in order for two reasons.

First, even those Council statements that repeat points already made by you do so in a different way and hence give a new look at them. In this way, they help summarize what went before.

Secondly, the texts selected will invariably include some aspects not previously treated and hence will contribute to a better knowledge of Me and My work.

Follower:

I'd like to begin with those texts that give an idea of Who You are, Holy Spirit, and what You do for the Church of Jesus.

1. Mission of the Spirit

"Christ sent from the Father His Holy Spirit, Who was to carry on inwardly His saving work and prompt the Church to spread out. Doubtless, the Holy Spirit was already at work in the world before Christ was glorified. Yet on the day of Pentecost, He came down upon the disciples to remain with them forever" (see Jn 14:16) (*Decree on the Missionary Activity of the Church*, no. 4).

"The Holy Spirit was sent that He might continually sanctify the Church, and thus, all those who believe would have access through Christ in one Spirit to the Father. He is the Spirit of Life, a fountain of water springing up to life eternal. To people, dead in sin, the Father gives life through Him, until, in Christ, He brings to life their mortal bodies" (*Constitution on the Church*, no. 4).

2. The Spirit and the Church

"The Spirit dwells in the Church and in the hearts of the faithful, as in a temple. In them He prays on their behalf and bears witness to the fact that they are adopted children.

"The Church, which the Spirit guides in the way of all truth and which He unified in communion and in works of ministry, He both equips and directs with hierarchical and charismatic gifts and adorns with His fruits.

"By the power of the Gospel He makes the Church keep the freshness of youth. Uninterruptedly He renews her and leads her to perfect union with her Spouse. The Spirit and the Bride both say to Jesus, the Lord, 'Come!'" (*Constitution on the Church*, no. 4).

3. The Spirit, Scripture, and Tradition

"*Sacred Scripture* is the word of God inasmuch as it is consigned to writing *under the inspiration of the Divine Spirit. Sacred Tradition* takes the word of God entrusted by Christ the Lord and the *Holy Spirit to the Apostles*, and hands it on to their successors in its full purity, so that led by the light of the Spirit of truth, they may in proclaiming it preserve this word of God faithfully, explain it, and make it more widely known.

JESUS SPEAKS OF THE HOLY SPIRIT—Jesus said to His Apostles: "If I do not go away, the Advocate will not come to you, whereas if I go, I will send Him to you. And when He comes, He will prove the world wrong about sin and righteousness and judgment" (Jn 16:7-8).

"Consequently it is not from Sacred Scripture alone that the Church draws her certainty about everything that has been revealed. Therefore, both Sacred Tradition and Sacred Scripture are to be accepted and venerated with the same sense of loyalty and reverence" (*Constitution on Divine Revelation*, no. 9).

4. Freedom Conferred by the Spirit

"The gifts of the Spirit are diverse: while He calls some to give clear witness to the desire for a heavenly home and to keep that desire green among the human family, He summons others to dedicate themselves to the earthly service of people and to make ready the material of the celestial realm by this ministry of theirs.

"Yet He *frees all of them* so that by putting aside love of self and bringing all earthly resources into the service of human life they can devote themselves to that future when humanity itself will become an offering accepted by God" (*Constitution on the Church in the Modern World*, no. 38).

5. The Spirit and the Missions

"The Holy Spirit uses diverse means to arouse the mission spirit in the Church of God, and ofttimes anticipates the action of those whose task it is to rule the life of the Church. Yet for its part, this office [of the Propagation of the Faith] should promote. missionary vocations and missionary spirituality, zeal, and prayer for the missions, and should put out authentic and adequate reports about them" (*Decree on the Missionary Activity of the Church*, no. 29).

Holy Spirit:

The texts you have chosen so far provide a good idea of My relation to the Church in general. There are other statements of the Council that go into greater detail about My relation to the Church and the People of God, for example, from the viewpoint of My influence on the holiness of Christians and their fulfillment of the duties of their states of life.

It might be well for you to recall these and so round out the entire picture.

Follower:

I see what You mean, Holy Spirit. Let me try to choose some texts that will reflect this point.

6. The Spirit and Faith

"To make [a free] act of faith, the grace of God and the *interior help of the Holy Spirit* must precede and assist, moving the heart and turning it to God, opening the eyes of the mind and giving joy and ease to everyone in assenting to the truth and believing it.

"To bring about an ever deeper understanding of revelation the same Holy Spirit constantly brings faith to completion by His gifts" (*Constitution on Divine Revelation*, no. 5).

7. The Spirit and the Laity

"For the exercise of the [Christian] apostolate, the Holy Spirit Who *sanctifies the People of God* through ministry and the Sacraments *gives the faithful special gifts also* (see 1 Cor 12:7), allotting them to everyone according as He wills (1 Cor 12:11) in order that individuals, administering grace to others just as they have received it, may also be 'good stewards of the manifold grace of God' (1 Pet 4:10), to build up the whole body in charity (see Eph 4:16).

"From the acceptance of these charisma, including those that are more elementary, there arise for each believer the right and duty to use them in the Church and in the world for the good of people and the building up of the Church, in the freedom of the Holy Spirit 'Who breathes where He wills (Jn 3:8).' . . .

"Lay persons should learn especially how to perform the mission of Christ and the Church by basing their life on belief in the Divine mystery of Creation and Redemption and by *being sensitive to the movement of the Holy Spirit* Who gives life to the People of God and Who urges all to love God the Father as well as the world and people in Him" (*Decree on the Apostolate of the Laity*, no. 3).

8. The Spirit and Married People

"Christian spouses have a special Sacrament by which they are fortified and receive a kind of consecration in the duties and dignity of their state. By virtue of this Sacrament, as spouses fulfill their conjugal and family obligation, they are penetrated with the Spirit of Christ, which suffuses their whole lives with faith, hope, and charity.

"Thus they increasingly advance the perfection of their own personalities, as well as their mutual sanctification, and hence contribute jointly to the glory of God." (*Constitution on the Church in the Modern World*, no. 48).

9. The Spirit and the Religious Life

"The adaptation and renewal of the religious life includes both the constant return to the sources of all Christian life and to the original spirit of the institutes and their adaptation to the changed conditions of our time. This renewal must be advanced under the inspiration of the Holy Spirit and the guidance of the Church" (*Decree on the Adaptation and Renewal of Religious Life*, no. 2).

10. The Spirit and the Priestly Life

"In order that, in all conditions of life, priests may be able to grow in union with Christ, they possess the exercise of their conscious ministry. They also enjoy the common and particular means, old and new, that the Spirit never ceases to arouse in the People of God and that the Church commends, and sometimes commands, for the sanctification of her members. . . .

"Nourished by spiritual reading, under the light of faith, they can more diligently seek signs of God's will and impulses of His grace in the various events of life, and so from day to day become more docile to the mission they have assumed in the Holy Spirit" (*Decree on the Ministry and Life of Priests*, no. 18).

"Holiness does much for priests in carrying on a fruitful ministry. Although Divine grace could use unworthy ministers to effect the work of salvation, yet for the most part God chooses, to show forth His wonders, those who are more open to the power and direction of the Holy Spirit, and who can by reason of their close union with Christ and their holiness of life say with St. Paul: 'And yet I am alive; or rather, not I; it is Christ that lives in me' (Gal 2:20)" (*Decree on the Ministry and Life of Priests*, no. 12).

11. The Spirit and Holiness

"It is not only through the Sacraments and the ministries of the Church that the Holy Spirit sanctifies and leads the People of God and enriches it with virtues, but allotting His gifts to everyone according as He wills. He distributes special graces among the faithful of every rank. By these gifts He makes them fit and ready to undertake the various tasks and offices that contribute toward the renewal and building up of the Church. . . .

"These charisma, whether they be the more outstanding or the more simple and widely diffused, are to be received with thanksgiving and consolation for they are perfectly suited to and useful for the needs of the Church" (*Constitution on the Church*, no. 12).

Chapter 34

THE FAMILY SPIRIT

Follower:

DEAR Holy Spirit, I would like to talk with You about the *Family Spirit*, the kind of Family that exists perfectly from all eternity in the Divine Family of Father, Son, and Holy Spirit. This is the spirit of which we find an expression in human terms in the Holy Family of Nazareth.

In it there was perfect peace, that is, tranquility of order, loving obedience of the Child, respect for authority, for "father" and mother, self-sacrificing love of husband and wife, of parents in relation to the Child, one heart and one mind.

There was a most intimate relationship with the Heavenly Father and with You, Soul of that family.

Holy Spirit:

You are right. The family spirit is something fundamental and it is all-important to teach and preach its necessity in season and out of season. This is especially true in this day when there are powers, diabolically inspired, that aim at destroying the human family as designed and willed by God, when some would like to introduce "free-love" (of the purely selfish kind), and when some mothers claim to have the right to murder their unborn children.

Man was created after the image of God and it is to be expected that the human family should also aim at mirroring the Trinitarian Family. As in the Trinity, so in the human family there is unity in diversity and the members of a human family should be of "one heart and one mind "

Follower:

I already see the "family spirit" as existing in what we like to call the "infant Church," which St. Luke describes as praying together during the Retreat before Pentecost. There we see Mary, Christ's mother, "Mother of God," who, though far surpassing St. Peter, is not governing the assembly.

We are familiar with the expression dear to Fr. Peyton: "The family that prays together stays together"; and this was true precisely of that large family, comprising Apostles, disciples, Mary, and her relatives, as St. Luke records it for us: *"All of these were constantly engaged in prayer"* (Acts 1:14).

We already recalled that You, Holy Spirit, provided inspiration through Your very special coming on the First Pentecost. You breathed in the members and in the converts a spirit of loving unity, a truly Christian family spirit. They became *one heart and one mind.*

Holy Spirit:

That loving spirit of unity was noticed by Jews and Gentiles who remarked on the Christians' love for one another. It became one of the reasons why many desired to join the true Church, which is God's family.

This is well expressed in Eucharistic Prayer I: "Father, accept this offering from Your *whole family*. Grant Your peace in this life. . . . Count us among those You have chosen."

Follower:

At this time, there is much talk about ecumenism, about the effort to bring about what Christ prayed for before His Passion and Death: *"That all may be one, as You, Father, are in Me and I in You; I pray that they may be [one] as We are one"* (Jn 17:21-22). However, it is important that there be unity in the Catholic Church *first* before there will be *unity* with the other Churches.

JESUS DESIRES AN END TO DIVISIONS—In His high priestly prayer, Jesus said: "Holy Father, protect by the power of Your Name those You have given Me, so that they may be [one], even as We are one" (Jn 17:11).

We must heal the divisions that exist in our own ranks—between "progressives" and "conservatives," between "professional-types" and "grass-roots" types, and the like. Only then—when we have a true *Christian Family Spirit*—can we expect non-Christians and non-Catholics to think about joining such a Church.

Holy Spirit:

You spoke of the Christian Family spirit and you did well. However, it is proper, as you have somewhat done, to point to the *eternal* Family spirit that manifested itself in the creation of human beings, not to speak of the creation of Angels who were destined to belong to the Divine Household, to be members of the Divine Family.

Why not broaden that reflection upon the family spirit as willed by God?

Follower:

It is easy to recognize that what stands out so clearly in Christianity is more than merely foreshadowed in what God initiated with our aptly termed first "parents." God could have chosen to create independent human beings with no more relationship or relations among them than what is found among varieties of stones.

However, God chose man and woman, husband and wife to generate children who depend for many years on the care of parents. We understand ever better that the parents are the first and fundamental educators and "upbringers" of children, called to bring them up not merely as children in the natural order but as adopted children of God, children of God for all eternity in heaven.

We know well that the family is the "cell" of the political "body," as it is the cell of the Mystical Body of Christ, the Church.

The Jews to whom Christ spoke realized that God was their Father, that they were children of God. But some objected when Christ claimed to be *the* Son of the Heavenly Father.

Holy Spirit:

Why not recall what the great Jewish convert Paul expressed so well in his Letter to the Ephesians?

Follower:

I thank You, Holy Spirit. How inspiring is that prayer of the Apostle of the Gentiles! Here is what he says and which the readers may like to read:

I kneel in prayer before the Father, from Whom all fatherhood in heaven and on earth takes its name. . . . May [He] grant through His Spirit that you be strengthened with power in your inner being and that Christ may dwell in your hearts through faith.

And I pray that, rooted and grounded in love, you may have the power to comprehend with all the saints what is the breadth and length and height and depth of Christ's love, and to know it even though it is beyond all knowledge, so that you may be filled with all the fullness of God (Eph 3:14-19).

Dear Holy Spirit, what a wonderful expression of the family spirit in relation to the Trinitarian Family!

Our misfortune is that we are so accustomed to using family terms, such as father, son, mother, child, etc., without growing in the true family spirit as willed by God, and as exemplified in Christ, Mary, and Joseph. Mother Church (that is what we call Christ's Mystical Body) is constantly using terms not only like Lord and God, but like Father and Son.

We have the expression that familiarity breeds contempt. It certainly did not produce that in the family of Nazareth. Familiarity with the Father, with the Son, and with You did not make Teresa of Avila impolite and, of course, did not generate contempt. Neither did the familiarity of Little Therese of Lisieux with Jesus, with the Father, and with You make her disrespectful.

On the contrary such familiarity made those great Saints ever more respectful, ever more self-sacrificing, always resembling more and more the loving spirit that You, Holy Spirit, pour into hearts.

Holy Spirit:

You know that mere reasoning about things does not automatically bring about a change in the wills of people. It is most important to advise them to *pray for a family spirit*. There used to be, for example, parochial associations called Holy Family Congregations or Societies.

Follower:

Yes, I remember, and when properly directed, they were instrumental in Christianizing family life. There still remains the *Feast of the Holy Family* celebrated on the Sunday in the Octave of Christmas, when the Church prays: "*Father*, help us to live as the Holy Family, united in *respect* and *love*. *Bring* us to the *joy* and *peace* of Your *eternal* home."

O God, send forth Your *Spirit* that families may be re-created, be spiritually renewed, and thus You shall renew the face of the Church.

Chapter 35

"NEARER MY GOD TO THEE"

Follower:

DEAR Holy Spirit, You have given me permission to hold a sort of conversation with You. What I have had in mind is that by such colloquies written down by me I might gain some inspiration not only for myself but for the readers of my notes.

You are always willing to come closer to us. And coming closer to You means coming closer to the Father and the Son. At the same time, we come closer to Your rational creatures, the Angels and human beings, who were created after God's image and likeness.

What struck me was that relations and relationships have existed from all eternity. Hence, through creation and especially through the Incarnation and Redemption, through all that the Father, the Son, and You, Holy Spirit, have done and continue to do for us, wonderful relations and relationships have multiplied.

From all eternity there was the relation between the Heavenly Father and the Son. From all eternity there was Your relation with both. There is a family relationship in the Holy Trinity.

In Nazareth there was the relation and relationship between Jesus become Man and Mary, the Mother, and Joseph the foster father and the husband of the Virgin Mother.

All that God did for Angels and for people was to bring them ever nearer to the Divine Family. One way of doing so is to bring human families and all individual persons and Angels nearer to the Family of Nazareth that is now forever in heaven.

Holy Spirit:

You do well not to try to entertain, or annoy, your readers with profound theologizing about the Holy Trinity. In this connection, you might recall a story about the great St. Augustine.

One day, while walking along the seashore, he was trying to fathom the Trinitarian mystery of Three Divine Persons in one God. He came upon a child who had dug a small hole in the sand and was bringing some water that he carried in a shell and then poured into the hole.

The Saint challenged the child regarding its foolish purpose, and the child answered: "It is easier to bring all the water of the sea and

put it into that hole than for you to understand fully the mystery of the Holy Trinity."

So, I repeat, it is a good thing for you to
deal with the subject of the relationships and
relations between human beings and the
Father, the Son, and the Holy Spirit. But you
did well in emphasizing that what God wants
is for His rational creatures who dwell upon
earth to come ever *nearer* to Him.

The way for them to do this is through the
many means put at their disposal for that purpose, such as prayer, the Sacraments, and the
Holy Sacrifice of the Mass—to mention just a
few of them.

Follower:

As I said at the beginning, relations existed
from all eternity. They exist in absolute perfection in the Holy Trinity. We creatures are nec-
essarily related to our Creator to Whom we
owe our natural human life. But God in His
unbelievable goodness wanted to establish
supernatural, that is "above-nature" relations
and relationships between us human beings
and God.

In the natural order, all human beings are
related to millions, to billions of things. They
are related to sun and moon and stars, to things

of earth, to fellow humans, and, above all, to God Who wants all to enjoy His presence, His beauty, His life, and share in His Blessedness forever.

What a sad thing it is that so many human beings today want to break off all relations with God and hence with eternal life with God, and make people be content with a short life of relationship with other people and with perishable earthly things. What a folly to try to make them enthusiastic about what is limited in time and in space.

How is it possible that some modern people, supposedly intelligent, reject relations with the Supreme Value: God, with the Divine Savior, with the Church that is appointed to help people to reach eternal family life with God. They thereby make people be content with purely earthly, temporal relations and relationships.

When Satan tempted our first parents, he did not propose to them to disobey God and thereby to be satisfied with a merely temporal earthly existence. He told them they would be like gods, something above their nature and something everlasting.

Holy Spirit, what is the best thing we can do, in the face of the spread of godless doctrines as well as the degeneration of religion in several countries, and the propagation of errors on all sides? How can we stem the tide of evil and error in the lives of those around us as well as in our own lives?

Holy Spirit:

You know the answer: Where there is error in the matter of religion, profess the true faith and live according to it. Where others do not pray, make sure that you pray. Imitate Christ without trying to perform miracles. Be always with Christ. Do all things for God's greater glory, for the sanctification of your own soul, and the sanctification of others.

Do all you can for the *spiritual* renewal of the Church. Be not human-centered but God-centered.

Follower:

I guess I could supplement this with something that is perfectly evident to You: Let us, by *following the Holy Spirit* in imitation of Jesus, Mary, and Joseph and countless Saints, stay close to our God.

I gave this colloquy the title taken from a hymn sung by the passengers of the so-called unsinkable Titanic: *"Nearer My God to Thee."*

Perhaps I can add here something that Fr. A. Lodders, C.SS.R., head of PRAYING NAZARETH, an association of Catholic Families, wrote some time ago:

"I asked a woman who is a celibate and whose father had died whether she did not suffer from loneliness after that bereavement. Here is what she answered:

" 'There are a number of people who have compassion toward me because I am living alone. But *I am not alone!* I have God with me. He dwells in me. If I did not have God, I then would certainly feel lonely and I would be oppressed by such a condition. But *He* is with me. He is in my company.

"'Believers in God who complain because of their isolation, their loneliness, should recall what we must believe, that God is present everywhere and that *He dwells* in those who love Him. In fact, after my work at the office, I like to be alone [with God]. People should not have compassion for me. . . . I enjoy being alone with God after a day of work at the office.' "

Thus ends the profession of faith of a Christian who lives according to her faith, who no doubt grows ever nearer to God, who, while retaining faithful relations with human beings, constantly strengthens her relations with God Who is our *All*.

Holy Spirit, teach us all to have a practical faith and hope in You, a practical love for You, and never to feel lonely, for we can and must say with St. Paul (Rom 5:5): *The love of God has been poured into our hearts through the Holy Spirit Who has been given to us.*

O God, You sent the Holy Spirit on Your Apostles. Grant us, who are Your people, the fruit of their loving prayers, that You may bestow peace upon those to whom You have given the most precious gift of Faith.

Holy Spirit, remain with us always, until we are safe in heaven with You, with the Father, and with the Son for all eternity. Amen.

NEARER, EVER NEARER, MY GOD, TO THEE!